THE BATTLE OF THE BULGE

WAYNE VANSANT

ZENITH PRESS

Quarto.com

© 2014 Quarto Publishing Group USA Inc.
Text and illustrations © 2014 Wayne Vansant

First Published in 2014 by Zenith Press, an imprint of The Quarto Group,
100 Cummings Center, Suite 265-D, Beverly, MA 01915, USA.
T (978) 282-9590 F (978) 283-2742

Zenith Press titles are also available at discount for retail, wholesale, promotional, and bulk
purchase. For details, contact the Special Sales Manager by email at specialsales@quarto.
com or by mail at The Quarto Group, Attn: Special Sales Manager, 100 Cummings Center,
Suite 265-D, Beverly, MA 01915, USA.

ISBN-13: 978-0-7603-4622-8

Library of Congress Cataloging-in-Publication Data

Vansant, Wayne.
  The Battle of the Bulge : a graphic history of Allied victory in the Ardennes, 1944-1945 /
Wayne Vansant.
    pages cm. -- (Zenith Graphic Histories)
  ISBN 978-0-7603-4622-8 (sc)
  1. Ardennes, Battle of the, 1944-1945—Comic books, strips, etc. 2. Ardennes, Battle of the,
1944-1945—Juvenile literature. 3. Graphic novels. I. Title.
  D756.5.A7V36 2014
  940.54'219348—dc23

                              2014012286

Editorial Director: Erik Gilg
Project Manager: Madeleine Vasaly
Design Manager: James Kegley
Layout Designer: Chris Fayers & Becky Pagel

Printed in USA

CONTENTS

ON THE EVENING OF FRIDAY, DECEMBER 15, 1944, IT WAS COLD AND QUIET ALONG THE WESTERN BORDER OF GERMANY. THE AMERICAN FORCES WHO HELD THE 85-MILE FRONT IN THE ARDENNES FOREST OF SOUTHERN BELGIUM AND NORTHERN LUXEMBOURG WERE CONFIDENT THAT TOMORROW WOULD BE JUST ANOTHER DAY THAT WOULD BRING THEM CLOSER TO CHRISTMAS. WHY WOULDN'T IT BE? TO THE SOUTH, GEN. GEORGE PATTON'S THIRD ARMY WAS BEGINNING A DRIVE INTO THE SAAR REGION. IN EASTERN EUROPE, THE RUSSIAN RED ARMY WAS NOW IN POLAND PREPARING FOR A MONUMENTAL OFFENSIVE DRIVE THAT WOULD CARRY THEM TO BERLIN. FOR ALL INTENTS AND PURPOSES, THE FORCES OF NAZI GERMANY WERE BEATEN, EVEN IF THEY DIDN'T KNOW IT YET.

BUT THAT NIGHT, JUST A FEW MILES AWAY FROM THE AMERICANS, BEHIND THE DEFENSES OF THE SIEGFRIED LINE, 250,000 GERMAN TROOPS, 1,900 PIECES OF HEAVY ARTILLERY, AND 970 TANKS AND ASSAULT GUNS WERE PREPARING TO LAUNCH THE LAST GREAT GERMAN OFFENSIVE OF THE SECOND WORLD WAR.

WATCH ON THE RHINE

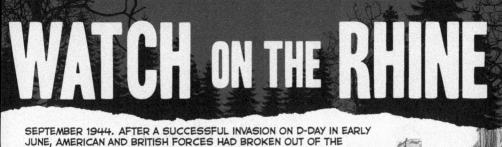

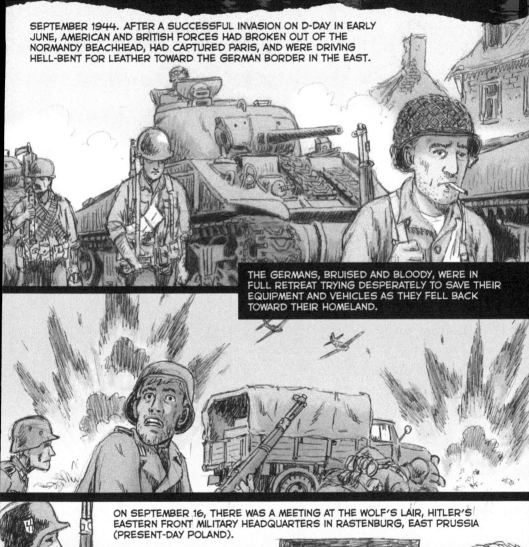

SEPTEMBER 1944. AFTER A SUCCESSFUL INVASION ON D-DAY IN EARLY JUNE, AMERICAN AND BRITISH FORCES HAD BROKEN OUT OF THE NORMANDY BEACHHEAD, HAD CAPTURED PARIS, AND WERE DRIVING HELL-BENT FOR LEATHER TOWARD THE GERMAN BORDER IN THE EAST.

THE GERMANS, BRUISED AND BLOODY, WERE IN FULL RETREAT TRYING DESPERATELY TO SAVE THEIR EQUIPMENT AND VEHICLES AS THEY FELL BACK TOWARD THEIR HOMELAND.

ON SEPTEMBER 16, THERE WAS A MEETING AT THE WOLF'S LAIR, HITLER'S EASTERN FRONT MILITARY HEADQUARTERS IN RASTENBURG, EAST PRUSSIA (PRESENT-DAY POLAND).

FIELD MARSHAL WILHELM KEITEL, COL. GEN. ALFRED JODL, AND COL. GEN. HEINZ GUDERIAN ARRIVED AT THE MEETING.

THEN ADOLF HITLER ENTERED THE ROOM. HE WAS HUNCHED OVER AND PALE, HIS EYES WATERY. HE SEEMED TO BE ONLY A SHADOW OF THE DYNAMIC LEADER WHO HAD TAKEN OVER GERMANY A DECADE BEFORE.

JODL BEGAN TO READ A REPORT ON THE CURRENT SITUATION ON THE TWO FRONTS. BASICALLY, THE GERMANS HAD FEW FRIENDS LEFT: MUCH OF ITALY HAD ALREADY BEEN CAPTURED BY THE ALLIES. ROMANIA AND BULGARIA HAD SWITCHED ALLEGIANCES AND JOINED THE RUSSIANS. FINLAND HAD SIGNED AN ARMISTICE WITH THE RUSSIANS. AND ALTHOUGH GERMANY STILL HAD 10,000,000 MEN IN UNIFORM, IT HAD LOST OVER 4,000,000 SINCE THE BEGINNING OF THE WAR—INCLUDING MORE THAN 1,200,000 CASUALTIES IN THE LAST THREE MONTHS, ALMOST HALF OF THOSE IN THE WEST.

THEN JODL MENTIONED SOMETHING THAT GOT HITLER'S ATTENTION.

ON THE WESTERN FRONT, WE ARE NOW GETTING A REAL REST IN THE ARDENNES. . . .

STOP!

HITLER STRAIGHTENED HIS SHOULDERS AS HE STARED DOWN AT THE MAP, HIS EYES BRIGHT AND ALERT.

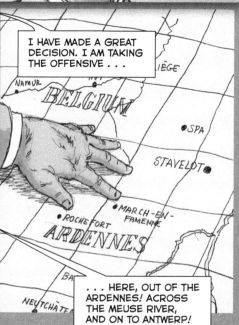

I HAVE MADE A GREAT DECISION. I AM TAKING THE OFFENSIVE . . .

. . . HERE, OUT OF THE ARDENNES! ACROSS THE MEUSE RIVER, AND ON TO ANTWERP!

THE NEXT DAY, SEPTEMBER 17, BRITISH FIELD MARSHAL BERNARD MONTGOMERY BEGAN A COMBINED AIRBORNE/ARMORED ATTACK ACROSS SOUTHERN HOLLAND TO CAPTURE GERMAN-CONTROLLED BRIDGES OVER THE RHINE RIVER. BECAUSE OF THE UNEXPECTED PRESENCE OF TWO GERMAN SS PANZER DIVISIONS, THE OPERATION FAILED MISERABLY.

THE ROAD INTO GERMANY PROVED MORE DIFFICULT THAN THE ALLIES EXPECTED.

BACK IN JULY 1944, A NUMBER OF HITLER'S GENERALS, INCLUDING COL. CLAUS SCHENK GRAF VON STAUFFENBERG, HAD TRIED TO ASSASSINATE HIM WITH A BOMB AT THE WOLF'S LAIR. AS A RESULT, HITLER'S CIRCLE OF TRUSTED CONFIDANTS HAD SHRUNK CONSIDERABLY. HIS PLANS FOR THE OFFENSIVE OPERATION HE PROPOSED, NOW CALLED WACHT AM RHEIN (WATCH ON THE RHINE), WERE DRAWN UP BY A FEW TRUSTED INDIVIDUALS.

I WANT THESE FIVE PANZER DIVISIONS WITHDRAWN FROM THE FRONT FOR REORGANIZATION AND RETRAINING . . .

. . . THEY WILL PLAY A KEY ROLE IN THIS OFFENSIVE.

WE MUST KEEP IN MIND THAT COMPLETE SURPRISE AND BAD FLYING WEATHER FOR THE ALLIES ARE ESSENTIAL.

GEN. RUDOLF GERCKE, WEHRMACHT CHIEF OF TRANSPORTATION, WAS ALSO KEY.

SUPREME COMMANDER OF ALL GERMAN FORCES KEITEL AND CHIEF OF OPERATIONS JODL WERE INSTRUMENTAL IN HELPING HITLER IN DRAW UP THE PLANS.

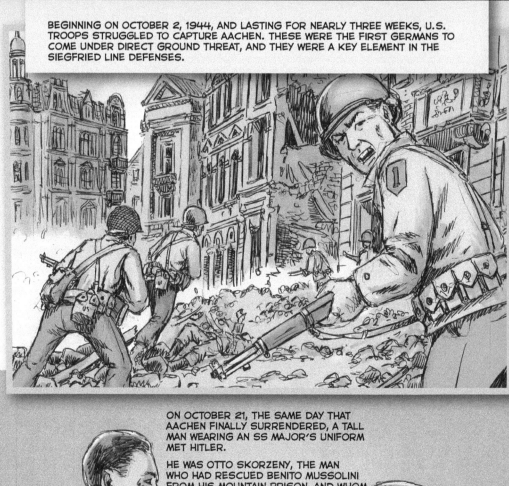

BEGINNING ON OCTOBER 2, 1944, AND LASTING FOR NEARLY THREE WEEKS, U.S. TROOPS STRUGGLED TO CAPTURE AACHEN. THESE WERE THE FIRST GERMANS TO COME UNDER DIRECT GROUND THREAT, AND THEY WERE A KEY ELEMENT IN THE SIEGFRIED LINE DEFENSES.

ON OCTOBER 21, THE SAME DAY THAT AACHEN FINALLY SURRENDERED, A TALL MAN WEARING AN SS MAJOR'S UNIFORM MET HITLER.

HE WAS OTTO SKORZENY, THE MAN WHO HAD RESCUED BENITO MUSSOLINI FROM HIS MOUNTAIN PRISON, AND WHOM BRITISH INTELLIGENCE CALLED THE MOST DANGEROUS MAN IN EUROPE.

I AM NOW GOING TO GIVE YOU THE MOST IMPORTANT JOB OF YOUR LIFE . . .

. . . IN DECEMBER, GERMANY WILL START A GREAT OFFENSIVE. IT MAY DECIDE HER FATE.

HITLER TOLD SKORZENY THAT HE WOULD TRAIN AND LEAD GERMAN SOLDIERS WHO SPOKE PERFECT ENGLISH TO MASQUERADE AS AMERICAN SOLDIERS. THEY WOULD WEAR AMERICAN UNIFORMS AND DRIVE AMERICAN VEHICLES AND WOULD CAPTURE BRIDGES, CHANGE ROAD SIGNS, AND SPREAD FALSE RUMORS AND PANIC IN THE AMERICAN REAR LINES.

AS THE PLANNING FOR WATCH ON THE RHINE CONTINUED, THE FIGHTING ON THE FRONT LINES GOT TOUGHER AND TOUGHER. IN NOVEMBER 1944, A NUMBER OF U.S. DIVISIONS STRUGGLED TO CAPTURE THE HÜRTGEN FOREST. THIS 50-SQUARE-MILE SECTOR COST THE AMERICANS MORE THAN 50,000 CASUALTIES AND THE GERMANS 28,000.

AFTER THE HURTGEN FOREST, MANY OF THE UNITS THAT FOUGHT THERE WERE SENT SOUTH TO REST IN THE LITTLE TOWNS OF THE ARDENNES.

HERE J.D. SALINGER WORKED ON *THE CATCHER IN THE RYE.*

BY EARLY DECEMBER, HITLER HAD THE WEATHER INFORMATION HE NEEDED:

SEVERAL EXPERTS FROM THE LUFTWAFFE HAVE PROMISED ME THAT BY THE MORNING OF THE 16TH, THERE WILL BE HEAVY FOG ALL OVER NORTHWESTERN EUROPE.

FINALLY, ON DECEMBER 11, HITLER BROUGHT IN HIS DIVISION COMMANDERS TO EXPLAIN WATCH ON THE RHINE. BEGINNING ON THE MORNING OF DECEMBER 16, THREE ARMIES WOULD BREAK THROUGH IN THE ARDENNES FROM MONSCHAU TO ECHTERNACH; THEY WOULD CROSS THE MEUSE RIVER AND REACH ANTWERP WITHIN A WEEK. THE AMERICANS AND BRITISH WOULD BE COMPLETELY SURPRISED BY THIS SUDDEN ATTACK AND WOULD BEG FOR A SEPARATE PEACE.

BOTH FIELD MARSHAL GERD VON RUNDSTEDT, COMMANDER OF GROUND FORCES IN THE WEST, AND FIELD MARSHAL WALTER MODEL, OVERALL COMMANDER OF THE OFFENSIVE, FELT THE PLAN WAS TOO AMBITIOUS BUT COULD NOT PERSUADE HITLER TO LIMIT THE MILITARY OBJECTIVES.

2ND INFANTRY DIVISION
VETERANS WHO CAME ASHORE ON THE DAY AFTER D-DAY, THEY ARE ATTACKING THROUGH THE 99TH TO CAPTURE THE ROER DAMS.

99TH INFANTRY DIVISION
CAME INTO THE LINE ON NOVEMBER 9. PATROL AND LIGHT COMBAT EXPERIENCE.

14TH CAVALRY GROUP
REACHED THE WEST WALL IN OCTOBER, AND TOOK UP POSITION IN BELGIUM ON DECEMBER 13.

106TH INFANTRY DIVISION
TOOK UP POSITION ON DECEMBER 11. NO COMBAT EXPERIENCE.

28TH INFANTRY DIVISION
VETERAN DIVISION, LANDED IN FRANCE ON JULY 22. SUFFERED HEAVY CASUALTIES IN THE BATTLE OF THE HÜRTGEN FOREST. IN THE ARDENNES TO REST AND REFIT.

9TH ARMORED DIVISION
GREEN DIVISION ARRIVED ON THE LINE IN OCTOBER. ONE PART OF THE DIVISION, COMBAT COMMAND R, IS ON THE LINE. THE REST IS IN AN AREA NEAR ST. VITH

4TH INFANTRY DIVISION
LANDED ON UTAH BEACH ON D-DAY, THEY ARE IN THE ARDENNES TO REST AND REFT AFTER HEAVY CASUALTIES IN THE HÜRTGEN FOREST.

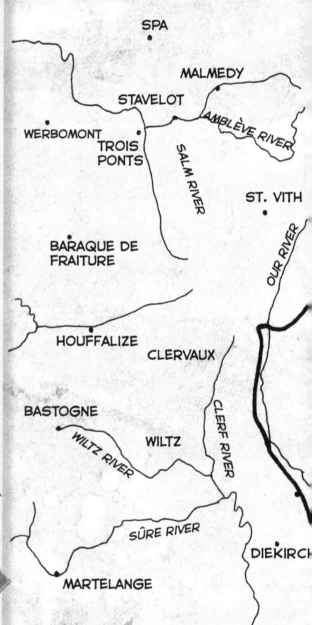

FRONT LINE THE NIGHT OF DECEMBER 15-16, 1944

EUPEN

MONSCHA

SPA

MALMEDY

STAVELOT

AMBLÈVE RIVER

WERBOMONT

TROIS PONTS

SALM RIVER

ST. VITH

BARAQUE DE FRAITURE

OUR RIVER

HOUFFALIZE

CLERVAUX

BASTOGNE

CLERF RIVER

WILTZ RIVER

WILTZ

SÛRE RIVER

DIEKIRCH

MARTELANGE

PRINCIPLE FORCES FOR "WATCH ON THE RHINE"

ROER RIVER

PRÜM

KYLL RIVER

PRÜM RIVER

BITBURG

6TH SS PANZER ARMY
COMMANDED BY ONE OF HITLER'S OLDEST COMRADES, JOSEF "SEPP" DIETRICK. DIETRICK WAS NEVER CONSIDERED A BRILLIANT MILITARY COMMANDER, BUT HE WAS IDEOLOGICALLY LOYAL TO HITLER, AND WAS A TOUGH VETERAN OF THE RUSSIAN FRONT. IN THE ARDENNES HE COMMANDED 4 PANZER, 5 INFANTRY AND 1 PARACHUTE DIVISION. DIETRICK'S ARMY WOULD SPEARHEAD THE ATTACK.

5TH PANZER ARMY
COMMANDED BY BARON HASSO VON MANTEUFFEL. COMING FROM A LONG LINE OF PRUSSIAN GENERALS, MANTEUFFEL WAS A BRILLIANT COMMANDER WHO HAD COMMANDED THE *GROSSDEUTSCHLAND DIVISION* ON THE RUSSIAN FRONT. ALTHOUGH JUST 5'2", HE WAS AN OLYMPIC ATHLETE. HIS 4 INFANTRY AND 3 PANZER DIVISIONS WOULD PIERCE THE LOSHEIM GAP AND CAPTURE THE ROAD CENTERS OF ST. VITH AND BASTOGNE BEFORE STRIKING TO THE NORTHWEST.

SEVENTH ARMY
COMMANDED BY ERNST BRANDENBERGER, A RELIABLE IF NOT GLAMOROUS SOLDIER WHO HAD SERVED WITH DISTINCTION. HIS ARMY WHICH WOULD PROTECT VON MANTEUFFEL'S LEFT FLANK AGAINST PATTON'S THIRD ARMY, WAS MADE UP MOSTLY OF INFANTRY DIVISIONS.

THIS BATTLE IS TO DECIDE WHETHER WE SHALL LIVE OR DIE. I WANT ALL MY SOLDIERS TO FIGHT HARD AND WITHOUT PITY. THE BATTLE MUST BE FOUGHT WITH BRUTALITY AND ALL RESISTANCE MUST BE BROKEN IN A WAVE OF TERROR. IN THIS MOST SERIOUS HOUR OF THE FATHERLAND, I EXPECT EVERY ONE OF MY SOLDIERS TO BE COURAGEOUS AND THEN MORE COURAGEOUS. THE ENEMY MUST BE BEATEN—NOW OR NEVER.

IN THE FINAL HOURS BEFORE MIDNIGHT, OFTEN ON ROADS COVERED WITH STRAW TO MUFFLE THE SOUND OF AN ADVANCING ARMY, 20 DIVISIONS MOVED UP TO THE FRONTLINES. THEY WERE ARMED WITH THE LATEST AND BEST EQUIPMENT: BRAND-NEW PANTHER TANKS AND THE HUGE 68-TON KING TIGER TANKS WHICH ALL ROLLED TOWARD THE FRONT.

I HAVE MY DOUBTS ABOUT THEM. THEY'RE TOO HEAVY FOR THESE NARROW ARDENNES ROADS . . .

JUST BEFORE MIDNIGHT ON DECEMBER 15, A SPECIAL MESSAGE FROM FIELD MARSHAL VON RUNDSTEDT WAS DELIVERED TO THE TROOPS.

"SOLDIERS OF THE WESTERN FRONT! YOUR GREAT HOUR HAS COME. LARGE ATTACKING ARMIES HAVE STARTED AGAINST THE ANGLO-AMERICANS. I DO NOT HAVE TO TELL YOU MORE THAN THAT. YOU FEEL IT YOURSELF. WE *GAMBLE EVERYTHING!* YOU CARRY WITH YOU THE HOLY OBLIGATION TO GIVE ALL TO ACHIEVE SUPERHUMAN OBJECTIVES FOR OUR FATHERLAND AND OUR FÜHRER!"

MEMORIES OF OLD VICTORIES FILLED THEIR HEARTS! IT WAS PAST MIDNIGHT. IT WAS NOW DECEMBER 16, 1944.

OPENING MOVES

THROUGH THE DARK, GHOSTLY FOG DURING THE EARLY MORNING HOURS OF SATURDAY, DECEMBER 16, INFANTRY FROM THE 5TH PANZER ARMY SILENTLY SLIPPED THROUGH KNOWN GAPS IN THE AMERICAN LINES. NONE OF THESE WAS MORE IMPORTANT THAN A 7-MILE-WIDE VALLEY CALLED THE LOSHEIM GAP.

THIS GAP WAS IMPORTANT FOR BOTH HISTORIC AND MILITARY REASONS. IT WAS THROUGH THIS VALLEY THAT GERMAN FORCES HAD POURED IN 1870, 1914, AND 1940. IT WAS THEIR NATURAL GATEWAY FROM EAST TO WEST.

BUT NOW, IN 1944, LOSHEIM GAP WAS AN IMPORTANT DIVIDING LINE BETWEEN TWO U.S. ARMY CORPS: THE VIII CORPS OF MAJ. GEN. TROY MIDDLETON IN THE SOUTH AND MAJ. GEN. LEONARD GEROW'S V CORPS IN THE NORTH.

GEROW'S MOST SOUTHERLY UNIT, THE 14TH CAVALRY GROUP, PATROLLED THIS AREA DAILY, KEEPING IN CONTACT WITH THE GREEN 106TH DIVISION TO THE SOUTH.

FOR A 2-MILE STRETCH, NOT A SINGLE AMERICAN OUTPOST OR FOXHOLE EXISTED.

THIS PUT TWO REGIMENTS FROM THE 106TH (THE 442ND AND 443RD) IN A VERY DANGEROUS POSITION. THEY HELD A LINE ON THE SCHNEE EIFEL (THE SNOW MOUNTAINS), WHICH STUCK OUT LIKE A FINGER ACROSS THE BORDER INTO GERMANY. THE HIGHER-UPS, GENERAL MIDDLETON AND FIRST ARMY COMMANDER LT. GEN. COURTNEY HODGES, THOUGHT IT WOULD BE A STRATEGIC POSITION WHEN THEY WERE READY TO ADVANCE INTO GERMANY.

BUT THE 106TH COMMANDER, 51-YEAR-OLD MAJ. GEN. ALAN JONES, THOUGHT HIS MEN COULD BE EASILY CUT OFF IF THE GERMANS ATTACKED.

FARTHER SOUTH, UNITS OF THE 5TH PANZER WERE SILENTLY CROSSING THE OUR RIVER TO FACE THE VETERAN, BUT DEPLETED, 28TH DIVISION.

ALTHOUGH VON MANTEUFFEL WAS BEGINNING HIS PORTION OF THE OFFENSIVE UNDER THE COVER OF SILENCE, "SEPP" DIETRICH WAS NOT. AT 0430, THE 6TH SS PANZER ARMY BEGAN THEIR ADVANCE WITH A THUNDEROUS BARRAGE.

FIRE!

THE SHELLS FELL AROUND THE MEN OF THE INEXPERIENCED 99TH DIVISION . . .

. . . BUT LUCKILY FOR THEM, THEIR POSITION INCLUDED BUNKERS AND LOG COVERINGS OVER THEIR TWO-MAN FOXHOLES, BUILT PREVIOUSLY BY BATTLE-HARDENED VETS. THE MEN IN THE 99TH HAD DONE NOTHING MORE THAN IMPROVE THESE DEFENSES.

THE 99TH MEN WERE SHAKEN, BUT FOR THE MOST PART THEY WERE SAFE.

AROUND 0700 (THE REPORTS VARY FOR DIFFERENT AREAS), THE CONSTANT BARRAGE STOPPED. FOR A WHILE, ALL WAS SILENT . . .

. . . THEN THE DARK SKY SUDDENLY LIT UP WITH A GHOSTLY GLOW.

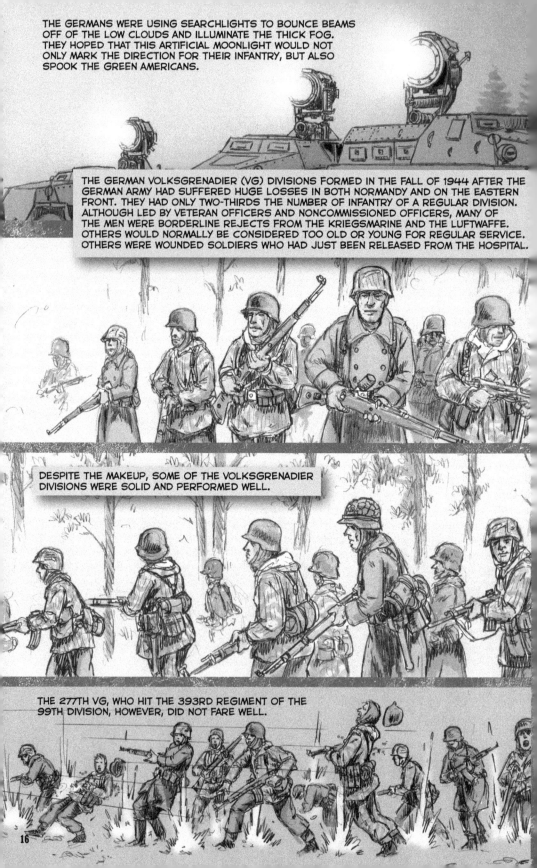

THE GERMANS WERE USING SEARCHLIGHTS TO BOUNCE BEAMS OFF OF THE LOW CLOUDS AND ILLUMINATE THE THICK FOG. THEY HOPED THAT THIS ARTIFICIAL MOONLIGHT WOULD NOT ONLY MARK THE DIRECTION FOR THEIR INFANTRY, BUT ALSO SPOOK THE GREEN AMERICANS.

THE GERMAN VOLKSGRENADIER (VG) DIVISIONS FORMED IN THE FALL OF 1944 AFTER THE GERMAN ARMY HAD SUFFERED HUGE LOSSES IN BOTH NORMANDY AND ON THE EASTERN FRONT. THEY HAD ONLY TWO-THIRDS THE NUMBER OF INFANTRY OF A REGULAR DIVISION. ALTHOUGH LED BY VETERAN OFFICERS AND NONCOMMISSIONED OFFICERS, MANY OF THE MEN WERE BORDERLINE REJECTS FROM THE KRIEGSMARINE AND THE LUFTWAFFE. OTHERS WOULD NORMALLY BE CONSIDERED TOO OLD OR YOUNG FOR REGULAR SERVICE. OTHERS WERE WOUNDED SOLDIERS WHO HAD JUST BEEN RELEASED FROM THE HOSPITAL.

DESPITE THE MAKEUP, SOME OF THE VOLKSGRENADIER DIVISIONS WERE SOLID AND PERFORMED WELL.

THE 277TH VG, WHO HIT THE 393RD REGIMENT OF THE 99TH DIVISION, HOWEVER, DID NOT FARE WELL.

ALTHOUGH THESE G.I.S WERE INEXPERIENCED AND GREEN, THEY HELD THEIR GROUND AND MANAGED TO THROW BACK EVERY ATTACK THE 277TH THREW AT THEM.

ANOTHER ELEMENT THAT HELPED THE 99TH'S DEFENSE WAS THE VETERAN 2ND INFANTRY DIVISION, WHO QUICKLY CALLED OFF THEIR ATTACK TOWARD THE ROER RIVER DAMS AND JOINED THE 99TH'S MEN IN THEIR LINE.

BY MORNING, THE GERMANS HAD NOT BEEN ABLE TO CAPTURE ANY OF THE ROADS DESIGNATED FOR THE PANZER'S MARCH. WHEN THE 12TH VG FINALLY CAPTURED ONE SECTION OF ROAD THEY NEEDED, THEY FOUND A RAILROAD OVERPASS THAT WOULD NEED TO BE REPAIRED BEFORE IT COULD BE USED.

FARTHER SOUTH, THE 12TH VG HIT THE 393RD'S SISTER REGIMENT, THE 394TH. THESE GERMANS MANAGED TO OVERWHELM THE BORDER OUTPOST AND CAPTURE THE VILLAGE OF LOSHEIM BY 0900 BUT WERE STOPPED COLD BY FOREST FIGHTING WITH THE 394TH.

BEHIND THE GERMAN LINE THAT DAY, MEN OF THE 1ST SS AND 12TH SS PANZER DIVISIONS WAITED IMPATIENTLY FOR THEIR INFANTRY TO OPEN A HOLE FOR THEM. "SEPP" DIETRICH WAS VISIBLY UPSET.

ON THE LOWER LINE OF HIS PANZER ARMY, GERMAN PARATROOPERS OF THE 3RD FALLSCHIRMJÄGER DIVISION WERE HAVING A DIFFICULT TIME WITH THE 14TH CAVALRY GROUP'S ARMORED CARS AND HALFTRACKS IN THE LOSHEIM GAP.

IN THE LOWER PORTION OF THE GAP, WHERE THE 5TH PANZER ARMY TOOK OVER, THE GERMANS WERE HAVING BETTER LUCK. VON MANTEUFFEL HAD OPTED NOT TO BEGIN THE OFFENSIVE WITH A MASSIVE ARTILLERY BARRAGE IN MOST OF HIS SECTORS.

BY SENDING IN INFANTRY TO QUIETLY INFILTRATE THE AMERICAN LINES, HE WAS ABLE TO SEND IN HIS PANZERS AT FIRST DAYLIGHT.

VON MANTEUFFEL SENT THE 18TH VG AND THE 244TH STURMGESCHÜTZ BRIGADE TO
ENCIRCLE THE TWO AMERICAN REGIMENTS OF THE 106TH DIVISION THAT HAD DUG IN ON
THE SCHNEE EIFEL. FROM THERE HE WOULD SEND HIS FORCES DIRECTLY WEST TOWARD
THE MAJOR ROAD CENTER OF ST. VITH.

ON VON MANTEUFFEL'S SOUTHERN FLANKS, THE MORNING ATTACK BEGAN WITHOUT
ARTILLERY PREPARATION. THE 116TH PANZER DIVISION AND THE 506TH VG DIVISION
HIT THE OUTNUMBERED VETERANS OF THE U.S.'S 28TH DIVISION.

20 MILES TO THE WEST LAY BASTOGNE. LIKE
ST. VITH, IT WAS A MAJOR ROAD CENTER.

ON THE FAR SOUTHERN END OF THE BATTLEFIELD, BRANDENBERGER'S SEVENTH ARMY,
COMPOSED OF INFANTRY AND A FEW ASSAULT GUNS, HAD ONLY PENETRATED ABOUT 4 MILES ON
THE FIRST DAY.

IF IT'S NOT A LOCAL ATTACK, WHAT KIND OF ATTACK IS IT?

WE'D BETTER FIND OUT. SEND TWO ARMORED DIVISIONS TO MIDDLETON.

AT SHAEF HEADQUARTERS IN VERSAILLES, DWIGHT EISENHOWER AND OMAR BRADLEY WERE INFORMED OF "ENEMY COUNTER ATTACKS AT FIVE SEPARATE POINTS ON THE FIRST ARMY FRONT."

BOTH EISENHOWER AND BRADLEY GRADUATED FROM WEST POINT'S CLASS OF 1915, A CLASS THAT EVENTUALLY PRODUCED 59 GENERALS AND WAS KNOWN AS "THE CLASS THE STARS FELL ON."

ONE OF THEM WILL HAVE TO COME FROM GEORGIE PATTON. HE WON'T LIKE IT.

BRADLEY COMMANDED THE TWELFTH ARMY GROUP, WHICH WOULD EVENTUALLY INCLUDE THE 1ST, 3RD, 9TH, AND 15TH FIELD ARMIES.

EISENHOWER WAS THE SUPREME ALLIED COMMANDER IN EUROPE. THOUGH HE HAD NEVER COMMANDED TROOPS IN COMBAT, HE WAS A BRILLIANT ADMINISTRATOR ABLE TO MAINTAIN HARMONY AROUND A COALITION OF MANY NATIONALITIES.

YOU TELL GEORGIE I'M RUNNING THIS DAMNED WAR!

THEY WERE RIGHT; PATTON DIDN'T LIKE IT. BUT HE SENT THE 10TH ARMORED DIVISION NORTH TO THE ARDENNES. EISENHOWER ALSO RELEASED THE ARMY'S ONLY RESERVES, THE 82ND AND 101ST AIRBORNE DIVISIONS, TO MEET THE GERMAN THREAT.

27 MILES NORTH OF THE ARDENNES AT THE U.S. NINTH ARMY HEADQUARTERS, BRIG. GEN. BRUCE CLARKE, COMMANDER OF COMBAT COMMAND B OF THE 7TH ARMORED DIVISION, WAS GETTING READY TO GO ON LEAVE TO PARIS.

GENERAL CLARKE. JUST GOT A CALL FROM GENERAL HASBROUCK. HE'S SAYS THAT YOUR PARIS LEAVE WILL HAVE TO WAIT.

BREAKTHROUGH

JUST HALF AN HOUR PAST MIDNIGHT ON DECEMBER 17, ELEMENTS OF THE 12TH SS (HITLER YOUTH) DIVISION EMERGED FROM THE WOODS ALONG THE SCHWARZENBRUCH TRAIL. THE MEN OF THE 99TH DIVISION HAD FOUGHT THEM EVERY INCH OF THE WAY.

AHEAD, ON A LOW RIDGE, WERE TWO SCATTERED VILLAGES THAT OVER TIME HAD GROWN SO CLOSE TOGETHER IT WAS NOW IMPOSSIBLE TO TELL WHICH WAS WHICH. THEY WERE KRINKELT AND ROCHERATH.

OR THE NEXT TWO DAYS, MIXED UNITS OF 2ND ND 99TH DIVISION MEN TRIED TO BLOCK THE GERMAN ADVANCE IN AND AROUND WHAT THEY OW CALL THE "TWIN VILLAGES."

FIRST LIEUTENANT JESSE MORROW, A TEXAN BY WAY OF NORTH CAROLINA, STALKED GERMAN TANKS WITH BAZOOKAS, RIFLE GRENADES, MOLOTOV COCKTAILS, AND A .45 PISTOL.

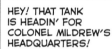
HEY! THAT TANK IS HEADIN' FOR COLONEL MILDREW'S HEADQUARTERS!

SOMEBODY GET ME A BAZOOKA!

OH, MY GOD! HE SEES ME!

HOW'S JESSE?

TANK SHELL GRAZED HIS NECK, BUT HE'LL LIVE.

AT 0300 ON THE MORNING OF DECEMBER 17, KAMPFGRUPPE (BATTLE GROUP) PEIPER WAS PREPARING TO ADVANCE. COMMANDED BY COL. JOCHEN PEIPER, THIS HEAVY PANZER GROUP, PART OF THE 1ST SS PANZER DIVISION, WAS THE SPEARHEAD OF THE 6TH SS PANZER ARMY. ITS OBJECTIVE WAS THE MEUSE RIVER.

REMEMBER, PEIPER, DRIVE FAST . . .

. . . AND HOLD THE REINS LOOSE.

PEIPER, AN ARDENT NAZI, HAD SPENT THE LAST COUPLE OF YEARS ON THE EASTERN FRONT OF RUSSIA AND HAD ONCE BEEN ADJUTANT TO SS CHIEF HEINRICH HIMMLER.

DRIVING HARD, PEIPER REACHED HONSFELD, ON THE OTHER SIDE OF THE LOSHEIM GAP, BY 0400.

WAIT! THERE'S AN AMERICAN FUEL DUMP 2 MILES TO THE NORTH AT BÜLLINGEN.

BUT WE'VE GOT ORDERS TO STAY ON THIS ROAD.

BUT PIEPER KNEW THAT FOR THE OFFENSIVE TO SUCCEED, THEY HAD TO CAPTURE EVERY DROP OF GAS FROM THE ENEMY.

MEANWHILE, SCATTERED UNITS BELONGING TO THE 7TH ARMORED DIVISION WERE ARRIVING FROM THE NORTH, HEADING FOR VIELSALM AND ST. VITH. ONE OF THEM WAS BATTERY B OF THE 285TH FIELD ARTILLERY OBSERVATION BATTALION . . .

THEY HAD JUST PASSED THROUGH THE TOWN OF MALMEDY, AND WERE NEARING THE LITTLE CROSSROADS SETTLEMENT OF BAUGNEZ.

AS BATTERY B REACHED THE BAUGNEZ CROSSROADS AT ABOUT 1300, THEY TURNED RIGHT TOWARD LIGNEUVILLE. SUDDENLY THEY WERE FIRED UPON BY TWO TANKS AND A HALF-TRACK ROLLING IN FROM THE EAST. THESE VEHICLES WERE PEIPER'S BATTLE GROUP.

THE AMERICAN TRUCKS AND JEEPS CAME TO A QUICK HALT, AND THE MEN JUMPED OUT AND TOOK COVER IN THE NEARBY DITCHES.

SOON, MORE GERMAN VEHICLES ARRIVED AND THE WAFFEN-SS MEN RUMMAGED THROUGH THE AMERICAN VEHICLES, YELLING AND LAUGHING LIKE CHILDREN.

THE MEN ORDERED THE G.I.S OUT OF THE DITCHES AT GUN POINT AND GATHERED THEM IN A FIELD NEAR THE CAFÉ BODARWE. THERE WERE ABOUT 100 OF THEM.

SS LIEUTENANT ERICH RUMPF WALKED OVER TO HIS MEN AND GAVE THE ORDER . . .

BUMP THE PRISONERS OFF!

THE PANZER GRENADIERS ALONG THE ROAD, IN HALF-TRACKS AND THE NEARBY TANKS, ALL OPENED FIRED ON THE AMERICANS.

THE MEN OF THE 285TH WERE CUT DOWN IN A HAIL OF BULLETS. MANY WERE KILLED INSTANTLY, SOME MERELY WOUNDED, AND A FEW NOT HIT AT ALL. SOME PLAYED DEAD, WAITING FOR A CHANCE TO RUN FOR THE WOODS.

THEN THE GERMANS STOPPED FIRING, AND THE ONLY SOUNDS WERE THOSE OF THE DYING. A FEW GERMANS WALKED AMONG THE WOUNDED AND SHOT THOSE THAT WERE STILL ALIVE IN THE HEAD.

A FEW WHO WERE NOT BADLY WOUNDED, OR NOT HURT AT ALL, MANAGED TO SLIP AWAY IN THE WOODS.

MORE THAN 80 U.S. SOLDIERS HAD BEEN KILLED. THIS EVENT WOULD BE REMEMBERED AS THE MALMEDY MASSACRE.

ON THE SAME DAY, NEAR THE BELGIAN VILLAGE OF WERETH, A GROUP OF 11 AMERICANS WAS HIDING IN THE HOME OF THE LANGER FAMILY. THE MEN WERE PART OF THE ALL-BLACK 333RD FIELD ARTILLERY, ATTACHED TO THE 106TH DIVISION, AND THEY HAD BEEN SEPARATED FROM THEIR UNIT DURING THE INITIAL GERMAN ATTACK.

LATE IN THE DAY, A GERMAN VEHICLE PULLED UP OUTSIDE THE HOME.

NOT WANTING TO PUT THE FAMILY IN DANGER, THE SOLDIERS WENT OUTSIDE WITH THEIR HANDS UP.

THE GERMAN SOLDIERS, MEMBERS OF THE WAFFEN-SS, RAN THE SOLDIERS DOWN THE ROAD IN FRONT OF THEIR VEHICLE UNTIL THE AMERICANS WERE TOO TIRED TO STAND.

THEN THEY PROCEEDED TO BEAT AND BAYONET THE 11 MEN TO DEATH.

SEVERAL WEEKS LATER, THE LANGER FAMILY, ON THEIR WAY TO CHURCH, FOUND THE BODIES PARTIALLY COVERED BY SNOW.

BRIGADIER GENERAL BRUCE CLARKE HAD NOW ARRIVED IN ST. VITH, BUT HIS COMBAT COMMAND B OF THE 7TH ARMORED DIVISION WAS STILL FAR BEHIND HIM. THEY HAD BEEN SLOWED DOWN BY RETREATING MEN AND VEHICLES OF THE 106TH DIVISION AND THE 14TH CAVALRY GROUP, WHO WERE MAKING AN UNAUTHORIZED DASH FOR THE REAR LINES . . . AND SAFETY. HE REPORTED TO THE 106TH DIVISION COMMANDER, MAJ. GEN. ALAN JONES.

YOU'VE GOT TO RETAKE SCHÖNBERG!

THE KRAUTS HAVE TAKEN SCHÖNBERG. THIS PUTS THE NAIL IN THE TRAP FOR MY MEN OUT ON THE SCHNEE EIFEL . . .

I CAN'T!

WHY NOT?

I CAME AHEAD. I DON'T KNOW WHEN MY MEN WILL ARRIVE.

CLARKE TOOK A LOOK AROUND ST. VITH. IT WAS AN UGLY TOWN. HALF THE RESIDENTS CONSIDERED THEMSELVES BELGIAN, THE OTHER HALF GERMAN.

ELEMENTS OF BOTH THE 6TH SS AND THE 5TH PANZER ARMIES WERE NOW POURING THROUGH THE LOSHEIM GAP. MAJOR DON BOYER OF THE 7TH ARMORED DIVISION WAS TRYING TO GET HIS MEN THROUGH THE HEAVY TRAFFIC RETREATING FROM ST. VITH. HE WAS ALSO BEING STOPPED EVERY FEW MILES BY MILITARY POLICE, WHO QUESTIONED HIM SUSPICIOUSLY.

WHO'S MICKEY MOUSE'S GIRL?

MINNIE.

THE BROOKLYN DODGERS. HEY, WHAT THE HELL IS GOING ON HERE?

WHO ARE DEM BUMS?

BOYER LOOKED MORE LIKE A COLLEGE PROFESSOR THAN A SOLDIER. HE GRADUATED FROM VIRGINIA MILITARY INSTITUTE IN 1938 BUT WAS ATTENDING THE FLETCHER SCHOOL OF LAW AND DIPLOMACY WHEN PEARL HARBOR TURNED HIM INTO A DIFFERENT KIND OF DIPLOMAT.

To the south, von Manteuffel's 2nd Panzer and Panzer Lehr Divisions had broken through the US 28th Division and were threatening Clervaux, headquarters of the 110th Regiment.

Breathtaking beautiful Clervaux had been a rest center. Consequently Colonel Hurley Fuller, commander of the 110th, gathered up all the officers and men at rest there to add to his 5,000-man regiment.

ON THE MORNING OF THE 17TH, LINES OF GERMAN TANKS REACHED THE HILLS TO THE EAST OF CLERVAUX, WHERE THE SWITCHBACK ROAD BEGAN ITS DESCENT INTO THE TOWN. CLERVAUX WAS SCHEDULED TO FALL BY NOON.

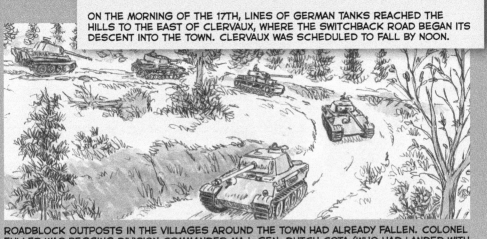

ROADBLOCK OUTPOSTS IN THE VILLAGES AROUND THE TOWN HAD ALREADY FALLEN. COLONEL FULLER WAS BEGGING DIVISION COMMANDER MAJ. GEN. DUTCH COTA (WHO HAD LANDED WITH THE 29TH DIVISION ON OMAHA BEACH ON D-DAY) FOR MORE ARTILLERY AND TANK SUPPORT.

I'VE GOT TWO OTHER REGIMENTS SCREAMING FOR HELP. I'LL SEND YOU A BATTERY OF SELF-PROPELLED GUNS.

IT'S ALL I CAN SPARE. AND REMEMBER YOUR ORDERS. NO RETREAT. NOBODY COMES BACK.

IT'S NOT ENOUGH!

ALTHOUGH THE GERMANS WANTED CLERVAUX BY NOON, COLONEL FULLER'S MEN WERE STILL HANGING ON AS NIGHT FELL. INFANTRY AND PANZERS WERE CUTTING AWAY AT ALLIED RESISTANCE IN THE CASTLE, HOTEL, CHURCH, AND HALF A DOZEN OTHER BUILDINGS.

JEAN SERVE WAS A YOUNG LUXEMBOURGER WHO HAD CARRIED AMMO AND DELIVERED MESSAGES FOR THE AMERICANS ALL DAY. IN THE CASTLE, HE HEARD PIANO MUSIC BETWEEN THE CRASHES OF SHELLS.

IN THE KNIGHT'S ROOM, AN AMERICAN SOLDIER WAS SITTING AT THE PIANO PLAYING CLAUDE DEBUSSY'S "REFLECTIONS IN THE WATER." A SHELL WOULD BLAST THROUGH THE WALLS, BUT THE SOLDIER DIDN'T MISS A NOTE.

THE GERMAN TANKS AND INFANTRY FLOODED THROUGH THE STREETS. THE COOKS AND THE CLERKS WHO HAD BEEN THROWN IN WITH THE VETERANS OF NORMANDY AND THE HÜRTGEN FOREST HELD THEIR GROUND AS LONG AS POSSIBLE.

IT SEEMED LIKE EVERYTHING IN CLERVAUX WAS BURNING. THE MEN AND TANKS OF THE 2ND PANZER ROLLED THROUGH, NOT WANTING TO WASTE A MINUTE. THEY HAD BROKEN THROUGH THE LINE. THE ENEMY HAD BEEN PUSHED BACK AND COULD NOT BE ALLOWED TO RECOVER.

BASTOGNE

THE ROAD TO BASTOGNE LAY OPEN.

BATTLE GROUP PEIPER

IN THE EARLY MORNING HOURS ON DECEMBER 18, A COLUMN OF VEHICLES FROM THE 14TH CAVALRY GROUP WAS AMBUSHED AND DESTROYED BY ELEMENTS OF THE 1ST SS PANZER DIVISION.

AFTER THE FIGHT, THE GERMAN TROOPERS TOOK TIME TO LOOT THE RAVAGED CONVOY OF FOOD, CIGARETTES, AND BOOTS, ALL RECORDED BY A GERMAN CAMERAMAN.

TO THE NORTH, ANOTHER COLUMN OF THE 1ST SS, KAMPFGRUPPE (BATTLE GROUP) PEIPER, APPROACHED THE TOWN OF STAVELOT. COLONEL PEIPER'S OBJECTIVE WAS TO CROSS THE AMBLÈVE RIVER AND THE AMBLÈVE GORGE, WHICH WAS NECESSARY TO REACH THE MEUSE RIVER.

4587

PEIPER'S MEN ENTERED STAVELOT AND FOUND A HODGEPODGE OF U.S. ENGINEERS, ANTITANK GUNS, TANK DESTROYERS, AND A LONE INFANTRY BATTALION, AN ADVANCED GUARD OF THE 30TH INFANTRY DIVISION.

AFTER A SHARP FIGHT, PEIPER'S TANKS CROSSED THE STONE BRIDGE. HE LEFT BEHIND SOME OF HIS MEN TO SECURE THE TOWN. HE THEN HEADED FOR TROIS PONTS.

THAT MORNING, A U.S. HALF-TRACK PULLING A 57MM ANTITANK GUN BROKE DOWN AT THE BRIDGE WHERE THE AMBLÈVE RIVER FLOWED INTO THE SALM RIVER.

HEY, COULD YOU GUYS SET UP TO COVER US WHILE WE PUT CHARGES ON THIS BRIDGE?

HIGH EXPLOSIVES DANGEROUS

SURE, WHY NOT?

IT IS VERY RARE IN MODERN WARFARE THAT INDIVIDUALS CAN MAKE A REAL DIFFERENCE AND TRULY CHANGE THE COURSE OF HISTORY. BUT THESE FOUR MEN—PFCS MCCOLLUM, HOLLENBECK, BUCHANAN, AND HIGGINS—WOULD DO JUST THAT.

PEIPER'S COLUMN HAD TO PASS THROUGH TWO BRIDGE OVERPASSES BEFORE IT COULD REACH THE SALM RIVER BRIDGE.

IT WAS HERE THAT THE ANTITANK GUN DID ITS JOB, HOLDING BACK PEIPER JUST LONG ENOUGH . . .

. . . FOR THE 51ST ENGINEERS TO BLAST THE STONE BRIDGE INTO THE SALM RIVER.

PEIPER WAS FURIOUS! HE SENT HIS TANKS FORWARD, DESTROYING THE DEAFENING ANTITANK GUN AND ITS FOUR-MAN CREW.

HIS ANGRY SOLDIERS ALSO DRAGGED 22 CIVILIANS FROM THEIR HOMES—MEN, WOMEN, AND CHILDREN—AND SHOT THEM ON THE RIVERBANK IN VIEW OF THE AMERICAN SOLDIERS ON THE OTHER SIDE.

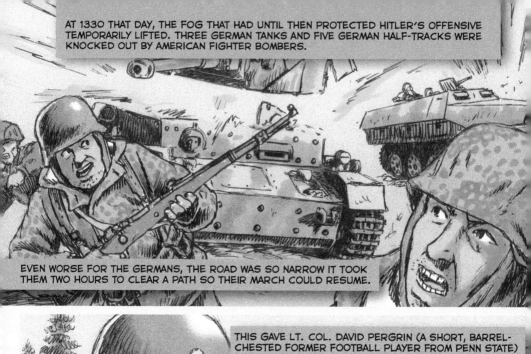

AT 1330 THAT DAY, THE FOG THAT HAD UNTIL THEN PROTECTED HITLER'S OFFENSIVE TEMPORARILY LIFTED. THREE GERMAN TANKS AND FIVE GERMAN HALF-TRACKS WERE KNOCKED OUT BY AMERICAN FIGHTER BOMBERS.

EVEN WORSE FOR THE GERMANS, THE ROAD WAS SO NARROW IT TOOK THEM TWO HOURS TO CLEAR A PATH SO THEIR MARCH COULD RESUME.

THIS GAVE LT. COL. DAVID PERGRIN (A SHORT, BARREL-CHESTED FORMER FOOTBALL PLAYER FROM PENN STATE) AND HIS 291ST COMBAT ENGINEERS TIME TO PREPARE THE NEUFMOULIN BRIDGE OVER LIENNE CREEK . . .

. . . AND BLOW IT UP IN PEIPER'S FACE.

THOSE DAMNED ENGINEERS!!!

THEY'RE TRYING TO HEM US IN.

WE'LL HAVE TO GET NORTH TO LA GLEIZE, AND THEN WEST TO STOUMONT .

PEIPER'S COLUMN REACHED STOUMONT ON THE MORNING OF DECEMBER 17, BUT THE U.S. 30TH INFANTRY DIVISION'S MEN AND TANKS WERE WAITING FOR THEM.

WE'VE GOT TO KEEP MOVING, MEN! TIME IS OF THE ESSENCE!

IN THE NARROW STREETS OF STOUMONT, AMERICAN MACHINE-GUN CROSSFIRE DEVASTATED PEIPER'S INFANTRY. AND AT CLOSE RANGE, THE HEAVY ARMOR OF THE GERMAN TIGER AND PANTHER TANKS PROVIDED LITTLE PROTECTION AGAINST THE SMALLER GUNS OF THE U.S. SHERMANS AND THE TROOPS' BAZOOKAS.

WE'LL PULL BACK TO LA GLEIZE AND DIG IN UNTIL OUR SUPPLIES CATCH UP WITH US.

BUT THOSE SUPPLIES WOULDN'T BE COMING. THE 30TH DIVISION HAD RETAKEN STAVELOT AND CUT PEIPER OFF FROM HIS REAR.

U.S. UNITS BEGAN TO CLOSE IN ON PEIPER'S BATTLE GROUP. ELEMENTS OF THE 3RD ARMORED AND THE 82ND AIRBORNE JOINED THE 30TH AND WERE SQUEEZING THE GERMANS INTO A POCKET AT LA GLEIZE.

ON DECEMBER 23, PEIPER REACHED HIS CORPS COMMANDER BY RADIO.

WE ARE TRAPPED WITHOUT FUEL OR FOOD, AND ALMOST OUT OF AMMUNITION. REQUEST PERMISSION TO BREAK OUT TO THE EAST.

REQUEST APPROVED IF YOU COME OUT WITH YOUR VEHICLES AND WOUNDED.

PEIPER KNEW THAT WAS IMPOSSIBLE.

DESTROY THE RADIO. WE'RE ON OUR OWN.

AT ABOUT 0200 ON THE MORNING OF DECEMBER 24, PEIPER LED WHAT WAS LEFT OF HIS BATTLE GROUP EASTWARD TOWARD HIS OWN LINES, LEAVING HIS TANKS AND 130 WOUNDED TO THE MERCY OF THE AMERICANS.

JUST AFTER DAWN, THESE 770 MEN REACHED FRIENDLY GERMAN LINES. PEIPER HAD LOST 70 PERCENT OF HIS MEN IN THE LAST WEEK AND ALL OF HIS HEAVY EQUIPMENT.

THE RACE FOR BASTOGNE

BY NOON ON DECEMBER 18, MOST OF BRUCE CLARKE'S COMBAT COMMAND B OF THE 7TH ARMORED DIVISION HAD REACHED ST. VITH AND THE BATTLE FOR THE TOWN WAS IN FULL SWING. HE WAS PLANNING TO ADVANCE EAST AND TRY TO BREAK OUT THE TWO REGIMENTS OF THE 106TH DIVISION TRAPPED IN THE SCHNEE EIFEL, BUT . . . . .

GERMAN FORCES ARE MOVING AROUND US TO THE NORTH . . .

. . . IF WE ADVANCE WE'LL BE EASILY CUT OFF. ST. VITH MUST BE HELD HERE!

GENERAL ALAN JONES WAS DESPERATE TO SAVE HIS TRAPPED REGIMENTS, BUT THERE WAS LITTLE HE COULD DO. TO THE SOUTH, AFTER CAPTURING CLERVAUX, VON MANTEUFFEL SENT THE 2ND PANZER, THE PANZER LEHR, AND THE 26TH VG DIVISION BARRELING TOWARD BASTOGNE.

SEVEN ROADS GO IN AND OUT OF BASTOGNE. THAT ROAD IS NECESSARY IF WE ARE GOING TO ADVANCE IN FORCE TOWARD THE MEUSE.

BASTOGNE

FAR TO THE WEST, TRUCKS FULL OF THE MEN OF THE 101ST AIRBORNE, WHICH HAD BEEN AT REST IN MOURMELON-LE-GRAND, FRANCE, WERE MOVING TOWARD THE BATTLEFIELD. MOST OF THEM HAD NO IDEA WHERE THEY WERE GOING.

TO THE EAST OF BASTOGNE, A FEW SCATTERED UNITS FROM THE 9TH AND 10TH ARMORED DIVISIONS WERE TRYING TO BLOCK THE GERMAN ADVANCE.

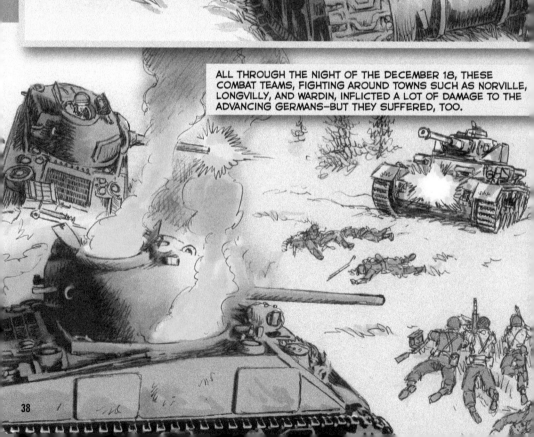

ALL THROUGH THE NIGHT OF THE DECEMBER 18, THESE COMBAT TEAMS, FIGHTING AROUND TOWNS SUCH AS NORVILLE, LONGVILLY, AND WARDIN, INFLICTED A LOT OF DAMAGE TO THE ADVANCING GERMANS—BUT THEY SUFFERED, TOO.

THE FIGHTS AT THESE ROADBLOCKS WERE HARD AND BLOODY.

I LOOKED FOR SMITTY, BUT ALL I COULD FIND WAS HIS HELMET . . .

. . . HIS BRAINS WERE IN IT.

THE 101ST COMMANDER, MAJ. GEN. MAXWELL TAYLOR, WAS IN WASHINGTON, D.C. LEADING THE DIVISION IN BASTOGNE WAS BRIG. GEN. ANTHONY McAULIFFE, THE DIVISION'S ARTILLERY OFFICER. McAULIFFE WAS A HARD-WORKING ARMY REGULAR KNOWN AS "OLD CROCK." REACHING BASTOGNE AHEAD OF HIS MEN, HE WENT STRAIGHT TO VIII CORPS COMMANDER MAJ. GEN. TROY MIDDLETON.

YOUR TROOPS WILL PROBABLY BE FIGHTING RIGHT HERE . . .

. . . I'LL BE MOVING MY CORPS HEADQUARTERS TO THE SOUTHWEST.

THAT NIGHT, THE FIRST ELEMENTS OF THE 101ST AIRBORNE PULLED INTO BASTOGNE. THEY WERE COLD, TIRED, AND SHORT OF EQUIPMENT AND AMMO.

FEW MEN HAVE OVERCOATS AND OVERSHOES. WORST OF ALL, WE'RE VERY LOW ON AMMO.

I'LL SEE WHAT MY MEN CAN PROVIDE AND WHATEVER WE CAN SCROUNGE.

AS THE FLOOD OF GERMAN FORCES FLOWED AROUND BASTOGNE, GENERAL EISENHOWER MET WITH HIS KEY COMMANDERS IN VERDUN, FRANCE.

THE PRESENT SITUATION IS TO BE REGARDED AS ONE OF OPPORTUNITY FOR US, AND NOT OF DISASTER . . .

GEORGE, HOW SOON CAN YOU TURN NORTH AND ATTACK TOWARD LUXEMBOURG AND BASTOGNE?

GEORGE SMITH PATTON III, AGE 59, WAS ONE OF THE OLDEST YET MOST HARD-CHARGING GENERALS IN THE U.S. ARMY. HE HAD PERFORMED BRILLIANTLY IN NORTH AFRICA AND SICILY, AND HIS THIRD ARMY HAD SPEARHEADED THE BREAKOUT FROM NORMANDY.

I CAN ATTACK WITH THREE DIVISIONS IN 48 HOURS.

DON'T BE FATUOUS, GEORGE. IF YOU TRY TO GO THAT EARLY, YOU WON'T HAVE ALL THREE DIVISIONS READY, AND YOU'LL GO PIECEMEAL.

I'LL GET THERE. I'LL ATTACK BY THE 22ND, AND NO LATER THAN THE 23RD.

THE 1ST BATTALION OF THE 501ST PARACHUTE REGIMENT MOVED OUT TO THE EAST AND AS THE FOGGY WEATHER ARRIVED, SO DID THE FIRST ELEMENTS OF THE GERMANS.

THE KRAUTS HAVE ARRIVED! DIG IN AND HOLD!

THE BATTLE FOR BASTOGNE HAD BEGUN.

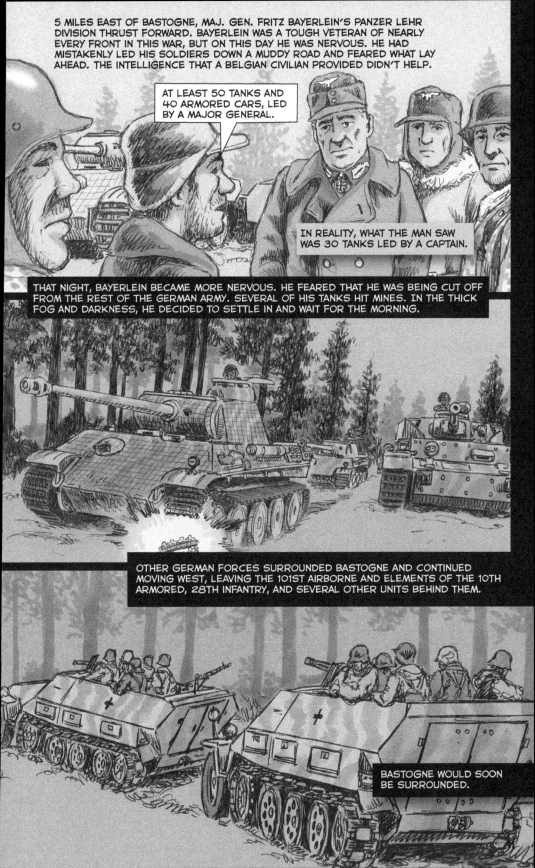

5 MILES EAST OF BASTOGNE, MAJ. GEN. FRITZ BAYERLEIN'S PANZER LEHR DIVISION THRUST FORWARD. BAYERLEIN WAS A TOUGH VETERAN OF NEARLY EVERY FRONT IN THIS WAR, BUT ON THIS DAY HE WAS NERVOUS. HE HAD MISTAKENLY LED HIS SOLDIERS DOWN A MUDDY ROAD AND FEARED WHAT LAY AHEAD. THE INTELLIGENCE THAT A BELGIAN CIVILIAN PROVIDED DIDN'T HELP.

AT LEAST 50 TANKS AND 40 ARMORED CARS, LED BY A MAJOR GENERAL.

IN REALITY, WHAT THE MAN SAW WAS 30 TANKS LED BY A CAPTAIN.

THAT NIGHT, BAYERLEIN BECAME MORE NERVOUS. HE FEARED THAT HE WAS BEING CUT OFF FROM THE REST OF THE GERMAN ARMY. SEVERAL OF HIS TANKS HIT MINES. IN THE THICK FOG AND DARKNESS, HE DECIDED TO SETTLE IN AND WAIT FOR THE MORNING.

OTHER GERMAN FORCES SURROUNDED BASTOGNE AND CONTINUED MOVING WEST, LEAVING THE 101ST AIRBORNE AND ELEMENTS OF THE 10TH ARMORED, 28TH INFANTRY, AND SEVERAL OTHER UNITS BEHIND THEM.

BASTOGNE WOULD SOON BE SURROUNDED.

THE FOG OF WAR

THE BATTLE SCENE AROUND THE TWIN VILLAGES OF KRINKELT AND ROCHERATH LOOKED LIKE SOMETHING FROM DANTE'S *INFERNO*. FIRE ILLUMINATED THE MANGLED WRECKS OF TANKS AND HALF-TRACKS, AND BODIES WERE STREWN ABOUT EVERYWHERE, BOTH AMERICAN AND GERMAN.

THE VETERAN 2ND INFANTRY DIVISION AND THE INEXPERIENCED 99TH INFANTRY DIVISION WERE DEFENDING THE VILLAGES, ALTHOUGH THE 99TH MEN WEREN'T GREEN ANYMORE. IN THEIR THREE DAYS OF COMBAT, THEY HAD PERFORMED WELL.

A FEW MILES BEHIND THEM, THE 2ND AND 99TH DIVISIONS, ALONG WITH THE 1ST INFANTRY DIVISION, WERE DIGGING IN ALONG THE LOW LINE OF HILLS KNOWN AS ELSENBORN RIDGE. THEIR OBJECTIVE WAS TO FORM A DAM OF MEN AND MACHINES TO STOP THE 6TH SS PANZER ARMY RIGHT IN THEIR TRACKS.

BY THE MORNING OF THE 19TH, THE BATTLE TOOK A DISTINCT FORM. POCKETS OF GERMAN ACTIVITY WERE POKING OUT INTO THE ARDENNES, AND AMERICAN UNITS SWARMED IN TO TRY AND STOP THEM.

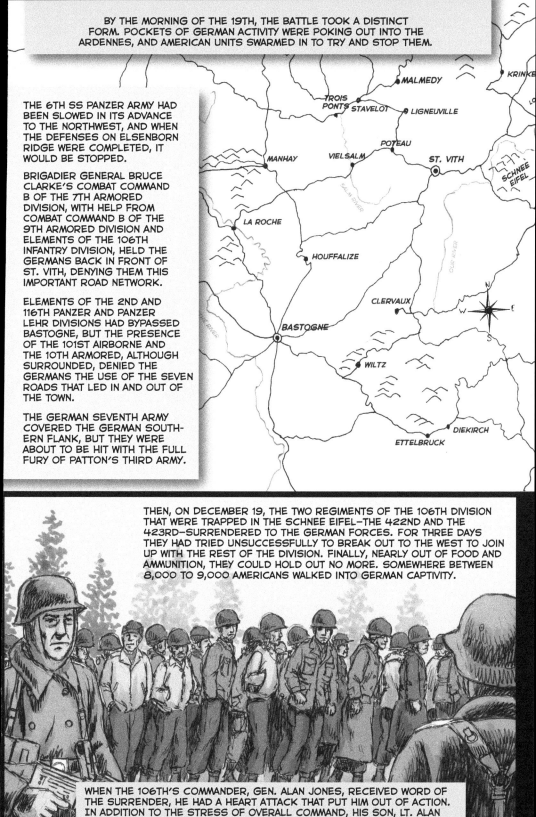

THE 6TH SS PANZER ARMY HAD BEEN SLOWED IN ITS ADVANCE TO THE NORTHWEST, AND WHEN THE DEFENSES ON ELSENBORN RIDGE WERE COMPLETED, IT WOULD BE STOPPED.

BRIGADIER GENERAL BRUCE CLARKE'S COMBAT COMMAND B OF THE 7TH ARMORED DIVISION, WITH HELP FROM COMBAT COMMAND B OF THE 9TH ARMORED DIVISION AND ELEMENTS OF THE 106TH INFANTRY DIVISION, HELD THE GERMANS BACK IN FRONT OF ST. VITH, DENYING THEM THIS IMPORTANT ROAD NETWORK.

ELEMENTS OF THE 2ND AND 116TH PANZER AND PANZER LEHR DIVISIONS HAD BYPASSED BASTOGNE, BUT THE PRESENCE OF THE 101ST AIRBORNE AND THE 10TH ARMORED, ALTHOUGH SURROUNDED, DENIED THE GERMANS THE USE OF THE SEVEN ROADS THAT LED IN AND OUT OF THE TOWN.

THE GERMAN SEVENTH ARMY COVERED THE GERMAN SOUTH-ERN FLANK, BUT THEY WERE ABOUT TO BE HIT WITH THE FULL FURY OF PATTON'S THIRD ARMY.

MALMEDY
KRINKE
TROIS PONTS
STAVELOT
LIGNEUVILLE
POTEAU
MANHAY
VIELSALM
ST. VITH
SCHNEE EIFEL
SALM RIVER
LA ROCHE
OUR RIVER
HOUFFALIZE
N
CLERVAUX
E
W
BASTOGNE
S
OURTHE RIVER
WILTZ
DIEKIRCH
ETTELBRUCK

THEN, ON DECEMBER 19, THE TWO REGIMENTS OF THE 106TH DIVISION THAT WERE TRAPPED IN THE SCHNEE EIFEL–THE 422ND AND THE 423RD–SURRENDERED TO THE GERMAN FORCES. FOR THREE DAYS THEY HAD TRIED UNSUCCESSFULLY TO BREAK OUT TO THE WEST TO JOIN UP WITH THE REST OF THE DIVISION. FINALLY, NEARLY OUT OF FOOD AND AMMUNITION, THEY COULD HOLD OUT NO MORE. SOMEWHERE BETWEEN 8,000 TO 9,000 AMERICANS WALKED INTO GERMAN CAPTIVITY.

WHEN THE 106TH'S COMMANDER, GEN. ALAN JONES, RECEIVED WORD OF THE SURRENDER, HE HAD A HEART ATTACK THAT PUT HIM OUT OF ACTION. IN ADDITION TO THE STRESS OF OVERALL COMMAND, HIS SON, LT. ALAN JONES JR., WAS AMONG THE PRISONERS.

WITH THE GERMAN DRIVE MAKING COMMUNICATION BETWEEN THE NORTHERN AND SOUTHERN SIDES OF THE BATTLEFIELD PROBLEMATIC, GENERAL EISENHOWER WAS FORCED TO MAKE A DIFFICULT DECISION: HE HAD TO ASSIGN EXCLUSIVE COMMAND TO SOMEONE IN THE NORTH WHO HAD THE CLOUT TO HANDLE IT.

THE ONLY PERSON WITH THE APPROPRIATE AUTHORITY AND STATUS WAS FIELD MARSHAL SIR BERNARD LAW MONTGOMERY, THE BRITISH MILITARY MAN WHO ACHIEVED FAME DEFEATING ERWIN ROMMEL'S AFRIKA KORPS IN NORTH AFRICA A FEW YEARS PRIOR.

THIS WAS A DIFFICULT DECISION, BECAUSE MONTGOMERY HAD BEEN CRITICAL OF MANY OF EISENHOWER'S DECISIONS AS WELL AS THOSE MADE BY HIS SUBORDINATES.

THERE HAD ALSO BEEN A PERSONAL RIVALRY BETWEEN MONTGOMERY AND PATTON SINCE THEIR TIME IN SICILY THE YEAR BEFORE.

EISENHOWER'S DECISION TO ASSIGN MONTGOMERY WOULD CAUSE MANY PROBLEMS AMONG THE AMERICAN CORPS AND DIVISION COMMANDERS, FOR THE BRITISH AND AMERICAN WAYS OF MAKING WAR WERE VERY DIFFERENT. MONTGOMERY WANTED TO WITHDRAW THE AMERICAN FORCES AND LET THE GERMAN DRIVE RUN ITS OWN COURSE BY RUNNING OUT OF GAS AND AMMUNITION. MONTY THEN WOULD WANT TO MOUNT A MAJOR OFFENSIVE TO PUSH THE GERMANS BACK TO THE SIEGFRIED LINE.

ALTHOUGH JUSTIFIED, EISENHOWER'S CHOICE ANGERED THE AMERICAN GENERALS OMAR BRADLEY, GEORGE PATTON, AND COURTNEY HODGES. THEY DIDN'T HOLD EISENHOWER PERSONALLY RESPONSIBLE, BUT BRADLEY NEARLY RESIGNED HIS POST. THE DECISION WOULD CAUSE AN EVEN GREATER CONTROVERSY LATER ON.

AFTER THE 101ST AIRBORNE REACHED BASTOGNE, GERMAN INFANTRY UNITS SEALED THE LINE AROUND THE TOWN, THEIR PANZER UNITS CONTINUING TO MOVE WEST ON THE SUBSTANDARD ROADS TO THE NORTH AND SOUTH OF THE TOWN.

GENERAL ANTHONY McAULIFFE SET UP HIS HEADQUARTERS IN THE OLD BRICK BARRACKS THAT THE BELGIAN ARMY HAD BUILT IN THE 1930S. THE BASEMENT ROOMS WERE PERFECT FOR ADMINISTRATION AND SUPPORT AND FOR AIDING WOUNDED SOLDIERS. WORKING WITH COL. WILLIAM ROBERTS OF THE 10TH ARMORED, THEY ORGANIZED THE DEFENSE OF BASTOGNE. WITHIN ITS DEFENSE PERIMETER WERE SCATTERED TROOPS FROM THE 28TH INFANTRY DIVISION AND THE 9TH ARMORED DIVISION.

WE'LL HAVE TO MAN A LIGHT PERIMETER, WITH FIRE TEAMS TO RESPOND TO HOTSPOTS.

YOU WERE SAYING THAT THINGS COULDN'T GET ANY WORSE?

LOW ON GAS AND AMMO IN ADDITION TO SUFFERING THE NEVER-ENDING SHORTAGE OF OVERCOATS AND OVERSHOES, THESE MEN FACED FEROCIOUS GERMAN ATTACKS DAY AND NIGHT. AND IT GOT WORSE WHEN IT STARTED TO SNOW.

45

TO THE SOUTH, PATTON GATHERED HIS FORCES TO DRIVE IN THE SOUTHERN SIDE OF WHAT IS NOW CALLED "THE BULGE." THESE FORCES INCLUDED THE 26TH AND 80TH INFANTRY DIVISIONS, BUT IN THE FRONT WAS HIS VERY ABLE 4TH ARMORED DIVISION.

BY NOW, ON THE NORTHERN SHOULDER, THE 2ND AND 99TH DIVISIONS HAD BEEN PULLED BACK, JOINING THE 1ST DIVISION IN THE DEFENSE OF ELSENBORN RIDGE. IT WAS A STRONG POSITION, BUT THE 6TH SS PANZER ARMY STILL BELIEVED THAT THEIR SECTOR WAS THE SHORTEST ROUTE TO ANTWERP.

THE 12TH SS PANZER DIVISION (THE HITLER YOUTH DIVISION) HAD SUFFERED HEAVY CASUALTIES IN THE FIGHT FOR THE TWIN VILLAGES, BUT THEY WERE STILL POWERFUL . THEY HIT THE U.S. 1ST DIVISION HARD AT DOM BÜTGENBACH, A LOCAL MANOR FARM.

FOR SEVERAL DAYS, FIRST IN HEAVY FOG AND THEN IN SNOW, THE 12TH SS WAS TURNED BACK BY BAZOOKAS, ANTITANK GUNS, TANKS, AND TANK DESTROYER FIRE.

THE 644TH TANK DESTROYER BATTALION SPREAD ITS 36 M10 VEHICLES ACROSS ELSENBORN RIDGE, ATTACHING THEM TO A HALF DOZEN DIFFERENT UNITS. THEY DID AS MUCH AS ANYONE TO HOLD THE LINE.

FINALLY, SEPP DIETRICH DECIDED THE U.S. LINE WAS TOO STRONG TO BREAK AND BEGAN TO SHIFT HIS UNITS LEFT, TO THE SOUTH, TOWARD VON MANTEUFFEL'S 5TH PANZER ARMY. VON MANTEUFFEL WAS MAKING SOME PROGRESS IN THE SOUTH, AND THERE WAS NO REASON THAT HE COULDN'T MAKE GOOD USE OF DIETRICH'S WAFFEN-SS MEN.

THE FIGHT FOR ST. VITH

THE FEAR OF OTTO SKORZENY'S SECRET GERMAN COMMANDOS, DRESSED AS AMERICANS AND SPEAKING PERFECT ENGLISH, WAS ON EVERYONE'S MIND. EVEN HIGH-RANKING MEN WERE STOPPED AND QUESTIONED UNDER GUNPOINT.

LIKE HELL! WE WERE TOLD TO LOOK OUT FOR A KRAUT DRESSED AS A ONE-STAR GENERAL.

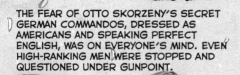

I'M GEN. BRUCE CLARKE OF CCB.

EVEN OMAR BRADLEY WAS STOPPED AND QUESTIONED.

MANY MILES TO THE SOUTHWEST, THE 5TH PANZER ARMY'S 2ND PANZER DIVISION WAS BYPASSING BASTOGNE TO THE NORTH AND HEADING TOWARD THE OURTHE RIVER. BELOW BASTOGNE, THE PANZER LEHR DIVISION WAS PASSING THE ROADBLOCK ON SECONDARY ROADS.

IF WE HAD TAKEN BASTOGNE AND ST. VITH, WE WOULD HAVE BEEN TO THE MEUSE BY NOW.

THE 116TH PANZER AND THE 2ND SS PANZER (MOVED DOWN FROM THE 6TH SS PANZER ARMY TO THE 5TH PANZER ARMY) WERE MOVING THROUGH THE AREA BETWEEN ST. VITH AND BASTOGNE.

ONLY SCATTERED U.S. INFANTRY UNITS, LIKE THE 112TH REGIMENT OF THE 28TH DIVISION, WERE THERE TO TRY AND STOP THEM . . .

. . . BUT TWO HEAVY UNITS WERE MOVING TOWARD THE BATTLEFIELD: THE 2ND AND 3RD ARMORED DIVISIONS, THE TWO BIGGEST TANK UNITS IN THE U.S. ARMY. THESE DIVISIONS WERE HEAVY ON TANKS BUT LIGHT ON INFANTRY, SO THE GREEN 75TH INFANTRY DIVISION WAS TO BE ATTACHED TO THE 3RD.

THE MAIN CONCERN FOR FIELD MARSHAL MODEL AND GENERAL VON MANTEUFFEL WAS ST. VITH'S DEFENDERS.

WE MUST GET CONTROL OF THE ROAD NET THERE, BEFORE THE AMERICANS CAN BRING UP THEIR HEAVY ARMORED DIVISIONS.

FUEL! THAT IS OUR PRIMARY PROBLEM. I MANAGED TO MOVE THE 9TH SS PANZER DIVISION HERE . . .

. . . AND WE FINALLY HAVE ENOUGH FUEL TO MOVE THE FÜHRER BEGLEIT BRIGADE HERE AT OBER-EMMELS.

THE FULL WEIGHT OF THE GERMAN FORCES WAS ABOUT TO FALL ON ST. VITH.

AMONG THE GERMANS, THE AVERAGE SOLDIER IN THE ARDENNES WAS IMPRESSED WITH THE MILITARY POWER THEY HAD UNLEASHED ON THE AMERICANS AND THOUGHT THEIR CHANCE OF VICTORY WAS VERY HIGH. "WHAT GLORIOUS HOURS AND DAYS WE ARE EXPERIENCING," ONE SOLDIER WROTE HOME. "ALWAYS ADVANCING AND SMASHING EVERYTHING! VICTORY WAS NEVER SO CLOSE AS IT IS NOW!"

WHEN THE FÜHRER BEGLEIT BRIGADE FIRST STRUCK AT THE DEFENDERS OF ST. VITH, THEY WERE QUICKLY "BLOODED" BY THE M36 TANK DESTROYERS OF THE 814TH TANK DESTROYER BATTALION. THESE VEHICLES MOUNTED 90MM GUNS THAT COULD TAKE OUT ANYTHING THE GERMANS HAD.

THAT SAID, ROBERT HASBROUCK, COMMANDING GENERAL OF THE 7TH ARMORED DIVISION, SAW THAT COMBAT COMMAND B WAS BEING ENCIRCLED.

GENERAL CLARKE, WE'VE ONLY GOT ONE LITTLE ROAD TO USE TO GET OUT OF THIS MESS.

IN THAT CASE, LET'S USE IT WHILE WE STILL HAVE IT.

SOME OF THE INFANTRY UNITS WERE ALREADY CUT OFF, AMONG THEM MAJ. DON BOYER'S.

BREAK UP INTO GROUPS OF FIVE AND TRY TO GET THROUGH.

I THINK IT'S TOO LATE, MAJOR.

BOYER'S CAPTORS WERE TOUGH, BUT UNDERSTANDING.

CHEER UP, MAJOR. IT'S JUST THE FORTUNES OF WAR . . .

. . . MAYBE I'LL BE A PRISONER TOMORROW.

HEY, WHO'S THAT?

THAT IS FIELD MARSHAL VON RUNDSTEDT.

NEAR MIDNIGHT ON THE 21ST, WAVES OF GERMAN TANKS WERE CLOSING IN ON ST. VITH.

WE'VE GOT THE WORD. WE'RE PULLING OUT. WE'RE TO FORM A LINE A MILE BEHIND ST. VITH.

THE TOWN OF ST. VITH BURNED IN THE DARK, THE SNOW FILTERING THE GLOW.

CHARLEY ONE TO CHARLEY SEVEN. WE ARE CLEARING ST. VITH.

WITHDRAW AND MEET US ON THE SOUTH SIDE OF TOWN.

A LONG COLUMN OF SHERMAN TANKS COVERED WITH INFANTRY AND A FEW GERMAN PRISONERS DROVE THROUGH THE SNOW, THE SOUND OF MACHINE GUNS BEHIND THEM. SOMEONE ON ONE OF THE TANKS STARTED TO SING.

SILENT NIGHT, HOLY NIGHT. ALL IS CALM, ALL IS BRIGHT . . .

A FEW OF THE GERMAN PRISONERS STARTED TO SING TOO. . . .

. . . SCHLAF IN HIMMLISCHER RUH . . .

NUR DAS TRAUTE, HOCHHEILIGE PAAR . . .

SIEGE BASTOGNE

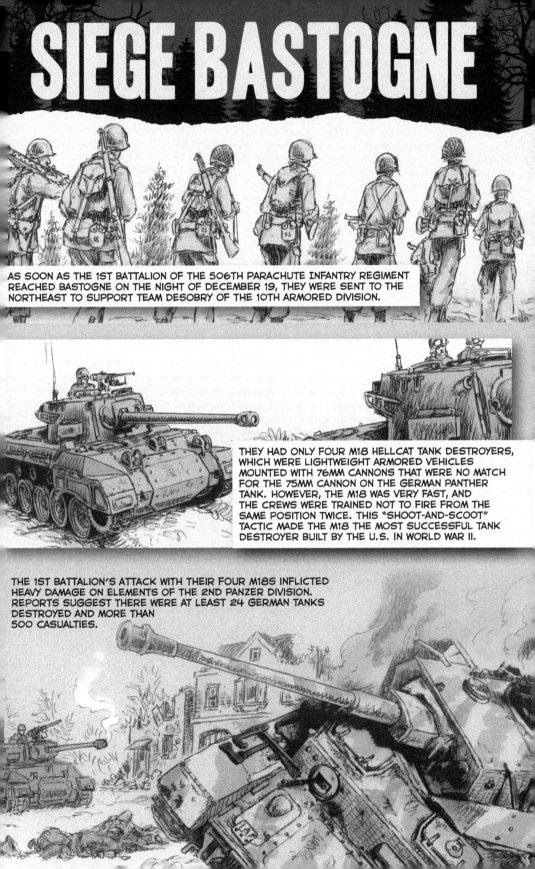

AS SOON AS THE 1ST BATTALION OF THE 506TH PARACHUTE INFANTRY REGIMENT REACHED BASTOGNE ON THE NIGHT OF DECEMBER 19, THEY WERE SENT TO THE NORTHEAST TO SUPPORT TEAM DESOBRY OF THE 10TH ARMORED DIVISION.

THEY HAD ONLY FOUR M18 HELLCAT TANK DESTROYERS, WHICH WERE LIGHTWEIGHT ARMORED VEHICLES MOUNTED WITH 76MM CANNONS THAT WERE NO MATCH FOR THE 75MM CANNON ON THE GERMAN PANTHER TANK. HOWEVER, THE M18 WAS VERY FAST, AND THE CREWS WERE TRAINED NOT TO FIRE FROM THE SAME POSITION TWICE. THIS "SHOOT-AND-SCOOT" TACTIC MADE THE M18 THE MOST SUCCESSFUL TANK DESTROYER BUILT BY THE U.S. IN WORLD WAR II.

THE 1ST BATTALION'S ATTACK WITH THEIR FOUR M18S INFLICTED HEAVY DAMAGE ON ELEMENTS OF THE 2ND PANZER DIVISION. REPORTS SUGGEST THERE WERE AT LEAST 24 GERMAN TANKS DESTROYED AND MORE THAN 500 CASUALTIES.

THE 101ST AIRBORNE'S FOUR REGIMENTS (501ST, 502ND, 506TH PIR, AND THE 327 GLIDER INFANTRY REGIMENT) FORMED THE PERIMETER AROUND BASTOGNE. WITHIN THE PERIMETER STOOD LIGHT AND MEDIUM TANKS OF THE 9TH AND 10TH ARMORED DIVISION AND FEW MEN FROM THE 28TH INFANTRY DIVISION WHO HAD BEEN CUT OFF FROM THEIR UNIT. THEY ESTIMATED THAT THEY WERE OUTNUMBERED FIVE TO ONE.

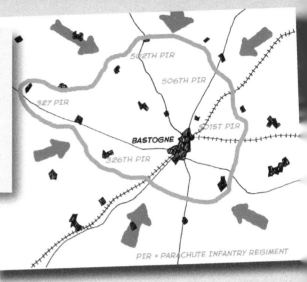

502TH PIR

506TH PIR

327 PIR

501ST PIR

BASTOGNE

326TH PIR

PIR = PARACHUTE INFANTRY REGIMENT

ELEMENTS OF THE 333RD FIELD ARTILLERY BATTALION, WHICH HAD BEEN PUSHED BACK FROM ITS POSITION ALONG THE GERMAN BORDER, ALSO WAITED WITHIN THE PERIMETER. THIS ALL-BLACK UNIT LOST MUCH OF ITS ARTILLERY BUT WAS LATER FOLDED IN WITH THE 969TH ARTILLERY BATTALION, WHERE THEY FOUGHT AS ARTILLERYMEN AND INFANTRYMEN.

FOR THEIR HEROISM, THE 333RD WOULD BE AWARDED A PRESIDENTIAL UNIT CITATION.

BY THE NIGHT OF DECEMBER 20, THE XLVII PANZER CORPS COMPLETELY SURROUNDED BASTOGNE, CUTTING OFF ALL SEVEN ROADS. THE U.S. MEN INSIDE THE PERIMETER WERE LOW ON FOOD, AMMO, AND WARM CLOTHING, AND THE FOGGY WEATHER HAD THWARTED THEIR HOPE OF BEING RESUPPLIED VIA AIR DROP.

ONCE THE PERIMETER AROUND BASTOGNE HAD BEEN SEALED, MOST OF THE GERMAN PANZER FORCES MOVED ON TO THE NORTHWEST IN THEIR DRIVE TO THE MEUSE RIVER. THE 26TH VG DIVISION AND ONE REGIMENT OF THE 15TH PANZER GRENADIER DIVISION REMAINED BEHIND TO TAKE THE TOWN.

THE 26TH VG WOULD PROBE SECONDS OF THE AMERICAN POSITION, MOSTLY ON THE WESTERN AND SOUTHERN SIDE OF THE PERIMETER. THEY WERE NOT STRONG ENOUGH TO MOUNT LARGE ATTACKS ON SEVERAL PLACES AT ONCE.

THEREIN LAY THE ADVANTAGE OF DEFENDING BASTOGNE. THE US FORCES HAD THE ADVANTAGE OF "INTERIOR LINES" AND COULD MOVE FORCES FROM ONE SIDE OF THE TOWN TO THE OTHER PRETTY QUICKLY. THAT SAID, THEIR TANKS AND TANK DESTROYERS HAD TO CONSERVE FUEL UNTIL THEY COULD GET RESUPPLIED, SO THEY WEREN'T AS NIMBLE WITHIN THE INTERIOR.

MEANWHILE, PATTON'S THIRD ARMY—HIS 4TH ARMORED, 26TH INFANTRY, AND 80TH INFANTRY DIVISIONS IN THE LEAD—WAS ADVANCING NORTH AGAINST THE GERMAN SEVENTH ARMY. THE GERMANS PUT UP A GOOD DEFENSE, BUT PATTON'S PRIMARY PROBLEM WAS THE WEATHER. MUDDY ROADS, SNOW, AND HEAVY FOG WERE NUISANCES, GROUNDING U.S. AIR SUPPORT AND LIMITING THE EFFECTIVENESS OF THE ARMY'S ARTILLERY.

WANTING TO GET GOD ON HIS SIDE, HE COMMISSIONED A "WEATHER PRAYER" FROM THE THIRD ARMY CHAPLAIN.

IT'S GOING TO TAKE A PRETTY THICK RUG FOR THAT KIND OF PRAYING.

I DON'T CARE IF IT TAKES A FLYING CARPET.

THE PRAYER WAS PRINTED ON ONE SIDE OF A CARD, WHICH WAS PRINTED AND DISTRIBUTED TO THE SOLDIERS OF THE THIRD ARMY.

PRAYER

ALMIGHTY and most merciful Father, we humbly beseech Thee, of Thy great goodness, to restrain these immoderate rains with which we have had to contend. Grant us fair weather for Battle. Graciously hearken to us as soldiers who call upon Thee that armed with Thy power, we may advance from victory to victory, and crush the oppression and wickedness of our enemies, and establish Thy justice among men and nations. Amen.

HEADQUARTERS
THIRD UNITED STATES ARMY

To each officer and soldier in the Third United States Army, I wish a Merry Christmas. I have full confidence in your courage, devotion to duty, and skill in battle. We march in our might to complete victory. May God's blessing rest upon each of you on this Christmas Day.

G. S. Patton, Jr.
G. S. PATTON, JR.
Lieutenant General,
Commanding, Third United States Army.

IN BASTOGNE, THE GERMANS CONTINUED TO HAMMER AWAY AT THE U.S. DEFENDERS. THE AMERICAN WOUNDED WERE TAKEN TO THE BASEMENT OF THE CHURCH OR TO THE BELGIAN ARMY'S BRICK BARRACKS.

TENDING TO THE WOUNDED SOLDIERS WAS 23-YEAR-OLD AUGUSTA CHIWY, A NURSE FROM THE BELGIAN CONGO. IN 2011, SHE WOULD BE AWARDED THE U.S. CIVILIAN AWARD FOR HUMANITARIAN SERVICE BY THE AMERICAN AMBASSADOR TO BELGIUM FOR HER SERVICE DURING THE BATTLE.

AT 1130 ON THE MORNING OF DECEMBER 22, FOUR GERMANS APPROACHED THE 327TH GLIDER INFANTRY. THEY HAD A MESSAGE FOR THE AMERICAN COMMANDER IN BASTOGNE. IT READ:

TO THE U.S.A. COMMANDER OF THE ENCIRCLED TOWN OF BASTOGNE.

THE FORTUNE OF WAR IS CHANGING. THIS TIME THE U.S.A. FORCES IN AND NEAR BASTOGNE HAVE BEEN ENCIRCLED BY STRONG GERMAN ARMORED UNITS.

THERE IS ONLY ONE POSSIBILITY TO SAVE THE ENCIRCLED TROOPS FROM TOTAL ANNIHILATION: THAT IS THE HONORABLE SURRENDER OF THE ENCIRCLED TOWN.

IF THIS PROPOSAL SHOULD BE REJECTED ONE GERMAN ARTILLERY CORPS AND SIX HEAVY A.A. BATTALIONS ARE READY TO ANNIHILATE THE U.S.A. TROOPS IN AND NEAR BASTOGNE.

ALL THE SERIOUS CIVILIAN LOSSES CAUSED BY THIS ARTILLERY FIRE WOULD NOT CORRESPOND WITH THE WELL-KNOWN AMERICAN HUMANITY.

THE GERMAN COMMANDER

COLONEL JOSEPH HARPER AND LT. COL. NED MOORE BROUGHT THE MESSAGE TO GENERAL McAULIFFE'S QUARTERS, WHERE THE GENERAL WAS SLEEPING. THEY WOKE HIM, AND WHEN HE READ THE MESSAGE HE SIMPLY SAID . . .

AW, NUTS.

McAULIFFE WENT ON ABOUT HIS BUSINESS, RUNNING THE DEFENSE OF THE TOWN. WHEN HE LATER RETURNED TO HIS COMMAND POST, COLONEL HARPER ASKED HIM . . .

SAY, TONY, THOSE KRAUTS ARE STILL AT MY COMMAND POST. THEY SAY THEY BROUGHT A FORMAL MILITARY COMMUNICATION AND THEY'RE ENTITLED TO AN ANSWER.

WHAT THE HELL SHOULD I TELL THEM?

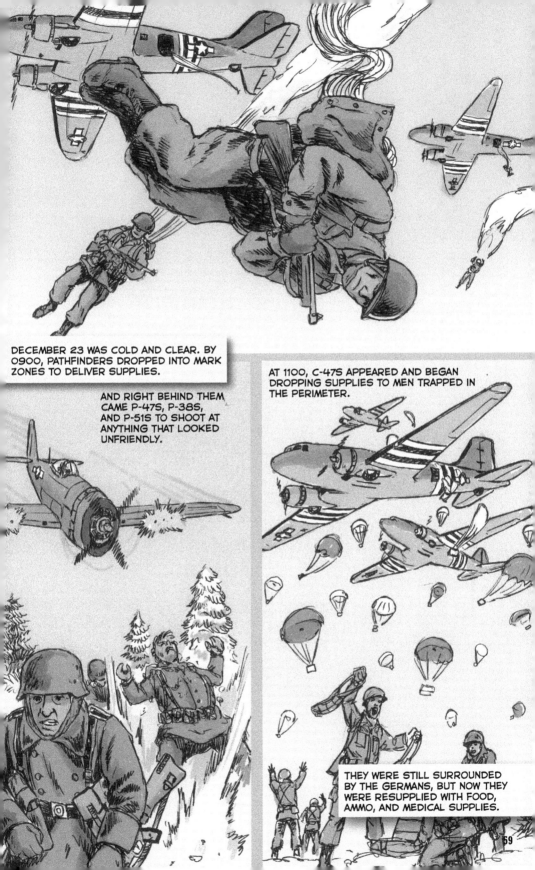

DECEMBER 23 WAS COLD AND CLEAR. BY 0900, PATHFINDERS DROPPED INTO MARK ZONES TO DELIVER SUPPLIES.

AND RIGHT BEHIND THEM CAME P-47S, P-38S, AND P-51S TO SHOOT AT ANYTHING THAT LOOKED UNFRIENDLY.

AT 1100, C-47S APPEARED AND BEGAN DROPPING SUPPLIES TO MEN TRAPPED IN THE PERIMETER.

THEY WERE STILL SURROUNDED BY THE GERMANS, BUT NOW THEY WERE RESUPPLIED WITH FOOD, AMMO, AND MEDICAL SUPPLIES.

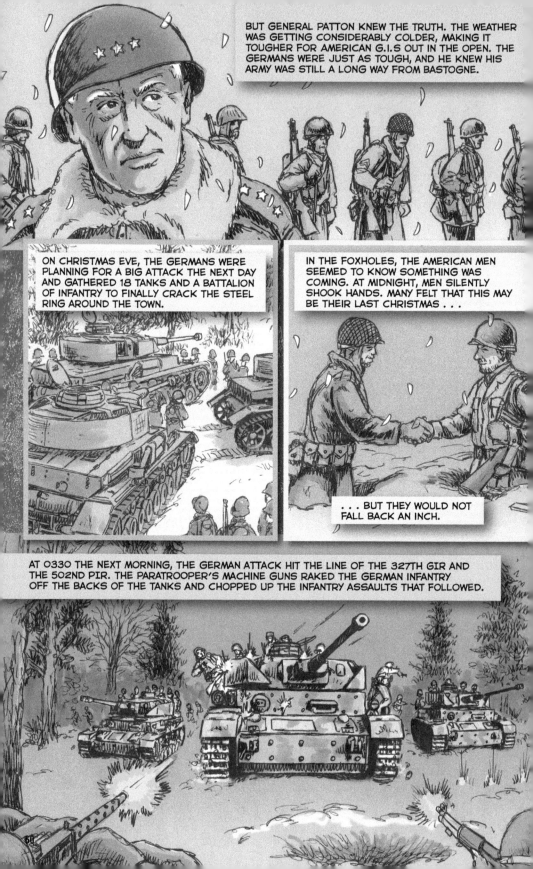

BUT GENERAL PATTON KNEW THE TRUTH. THE WEATHER WAS GETTING CONSIDERABLY COLDER, MAKING IT TOUGHER FOR AMERICAN G.I.S OUT IN THE OPEN. THE GERMANS WERE JUST AS TOUGH, AND HE KNEW HIS ARMY WAS STILL A LONG WAY FROM BASTOGNE.

ON CHRISTMAS EVE, THE GERMANS WERE PLANNING FOR A BIG ATTACK THE NEXT DAY AND GATHERED 18 TANKS AND A BATTALION OF INFANTRY TO FINALLY CRACK THE STEEL RING AROUND THE TOWN.

IN THE FOXHOLES, THE AMERICAN MEN SEEMED TO KNOW SOMETHING WAS COMING. AT MIDNIGHT, MEN SILENTLY SHOOK HANDS. MANY FELT THAT THIS MAY BE THEIR LAST CHRISTMAS . . .

. . . BUT THEY WOULD NOT FALL BACK AN INCH.

AT 0330 THE NEXT MORNING, THE GERMAN ATTACK HIT THE LINE OF THE 327TH GIR AND THE 502ND PIR. THE PARATROOPER'S MACHINE GUNS RAKED THE GERMAN INFANTRY OFF THE BACKS OF THE TANKS AND CHOPPED UP THE INFANTRY ASSAULTS THAT FOLLOWED.

WITHOUT THEIR INFANTRY TO SUPPORT THEM, THE GERMAN TANKS ADVANCED TOWARD THE BATTALION HEADQUARTERS AT HEMROULLE. MANY GERMAN TANKS WERE KNOCKED OUT BY BAZOOKAMEN OF THE 502ND . . .

. . . AND THE REST BY M18S OF THE 705TH TANK DESTROYER BATTALION.

THE NEWS OF THE STUBBORN STAND OF THE 101ST AT BASTOGNE SOON SPREAD ACROSS THE ARDENNES AND BOOSTED THE MORAL OF EVERY AMERICAN G.I.

BUT FARTHER WEST, THE GERMANS CONTINUED THEIR ADVANCE TOWARD THE MEUSE RIVER.

ALTHOUGH THE 7TH ARMORED DIVISION AND ITS ATTACHED UNITS WERE PUSHED OUT OF ST. VITH LATE ON THE NIGHT OF DECEMBER 21, THE MEN WERE STILL IN GREAT DANGER. THEY WERE IN A ROUND POCKET, CALLED "THE FORTIFIED GOOSE EGG." THEIR ONLY ROUTE OF ESCAPE WAS JUST 3 MILES WIDE.

VIELSALM

SALMCHATEAU

ST.VITH

THE PROBLEM WE HAVE IS THAT THE ROADS ARE SO MUDDY, OUR TANKS CAN'T MOVE ON THEM . . .

. . . IF THE TEMPERATURE WOULD DROP A LITTLE, THE ROADS WOULD FREEZE AND WE'D BE OKAY.

MAJ. GEN. MATTHEW RIDGWAY, COMMANDER OF THE XVIII AIRBORNE CORPS, NOW RECEIVED THE 7TH ARMORED AS WELL (RIDGWAY WOULD LATER COMMAND ALL UNITED NATIONS TROOPS IN THE KOREAN WAR). HE WANTED THEM PULLED OUT OF THE "GOOSE EGG" AS SOON AS POSSIBLE.

IT WOULD BE EARLY THE NEXT MORNING BEFORE A HARD FREEZE CAME ALONG.

A LINE STARTED FORMING TO THE WEST. THE GERMAN DRIVE WAS SWINGING LIKE A DOOR, WITH THE HINGE AT ELSENBORN RIDGE. VON MANTEUFFEL WAS SHIFTING HIS UNITS WEST, HOPING TO CIRCLE HIS UNITS TO THE LEFT AROUND THE AMERICAN FLANK. THE AMERICANS, SEEING THIS, BROUGHT IN UNITS FROM WHEREVER THEY COULD TO BLOCK THEM.

82ND AIRBORNE DIVISION

STAVELOT

7TH ARMORED DIVISION

3RD ARMORED DIVISION

75TH INFANTRY DIVISION

3RD ARMORED DIVISION

VIELSALM

ST

2ND ARMORED DIVISION

CINEY

HOTTEN

MANHAY

DINANT

84TH INFANTRY DIVISION

CONNEUX

CELLES

MARCHE

BARAQUE DE FRAITURE

2ND SS PANZER DIVISION

LA ROCHE

BANDE

ROCHEFORT

2ND PAN DIVISI

116TH

TO THE WEST OF RIDGWAY WAS THE VII CORPS OF MAJ. GEN. J. LAWTON COLLINS, WHICH CONSISTED OF THE 2ND AND 3RD ARMORED DIVISIONS AND THE 75TH, 83RD, AND 84TH INFANTRY DIVISIONS.

PANZER LEHR DIVISION

MAJOR ARTHUR PARKER III, AN ARTILLERY OFFICER WITH THE 106TH DIVISION, HAD ANOTHER ODD ASSIGNMENT. ON DECEMBER 19, HE WAS ORDERED TO TAKE THREE 105MM HOWITZERS TO THE LITTLE CROSSROADS OF BARAQUE DE FRAITURE AND SET UP A ROADBLOCK.

WHEN HE GOT THERE, HE STUDIED THE ROAD MAP AND REALIZED HOW IMPORTANT THIS TINY CROSSROADS WAS. IT WAS ON A KEY ROUTE TO THE NORTHWEST FROM BASTOGNE TO LIEGE.

HE MANAGED TO CONVINCE SEVERAL OTHER PASSING UNITS TO JOIN HIM: AN ANTI-AIRCRAFT UNIT WITH HALF-TRACKS MOUNTING QUAD .50-CALIBERS, A SELF-PROPELLED 37MM, A RECONNAISSANCE COMPANY FROM THE 7TH ARMORED, TWO M5 STUART TANKS, AND SEVERAL DOZEN STRAGGLERS.

PARKER SET UP HIS DEFENSES WITH THE UNITS AT HAND . . . AND THEN HE WAITED.

EARLY ON THE MORNING OF DECEMBER 21, PARKER'S MEN
SPOTTED AN 80-MAN GERMAN PATROL COMING UP THE ROAD FROM
HOUFFALIZE TO THE SOUTH. THE ROAD WAS STRAIGHT WITH LARGE
OPEN FIELDS ON BOTH SIDES.

THE FOUR ANTI-AIRCRAFT HALF-TRACKS OPENED
UP WITH THEIR QUAD .50-CALIBERS . . .

. . . AND CUT THE PATROL TO PIECES.

WHEN IT WAS OVER, SOME OF PARKER'S MEN CHECKED OUT THE BODIES
AND FOUND THAT MOST OF THEM WERE MEN OF THE 560TH VG DIVISION, BUT
AMONG THEM WAS AN OFFICER FROM THE 2ND SS PANZER DIVISION.

A COMPANY OF GLIDER INFANTRY FROM
THE 82ND AIRBORNE WAS SENT TO SHORE
UP THE ROADBLOCK ON THE 22ND.

AS J. LAWTON COLLINS BROUGHT IN HIS DIVISIONS TO FACE THE GERMAN ADVANCE, MONTGOMERY, THE OVERALL COMMANDER, WARNED HIM TO AVOID CONTACT. MONTGOMERY SUGGESTED LETTING THE GERMANS ADVANCE, FALLING BACK IF NECESSARY, AND THEN THERE WOULD BE NO COUNTERATTACK UNTIL THE GERMAN OFFENSIVE HAD RUN ITS COURSE.

THIS STRATEGY MADE NO SENSE TO COLLINS, WHO HAD COMMANDED A BATTALION IN WORLD WAR I AND WOULD GO ON TO SERVE AS THE U.S. ARMY'S CHIEF OF STAFF.

BUT FOR THE TIME BEING, IT WAS FINE WITH MAJ. GEN. ERNEST "OLD GRAVEL VOICE" HARMON, COMMANDER OF THE 2ND ARMORED DIVISION.

MONTY WANTS YOU TO LIE LOW FOR A WHILE AND GET READY FOR A SURPRISE COUNTERATTACK.

THAT'S FINE WITH ME.

I'VE GOT 14,000 MIGHTY TIRED BOYS.

WE PULLED OUT OF HEAVY FIGHTING AND MOVED 70 MILES OVERNIGHT TO GET HERE. . . .

HARMON WAS A BATTLE-HARDENED TANK SOLDIER WHO HAD FOUGHT IN NORTH AFRICA, SICILY, AND NORMANDY.

HE WENT BACK TO HIS HEADQUARTERS AT MARCHE AND WAS HAVING LUNCH WITH HIS OFFICERS WHEN LT. EVERETT JONES BURST IN WITH A BANDAGE ON HIS HEAD.

MY PATROL WAS FIRED ON, SIR. THEY HAD AT LEAST TWO MARK IV TANKS. . . THE KRAUTS ARE JUST 10 MILES AWAY AND THEY'RE COMING LIKE HELL!

AT BARAQUE DE FRAITURE, THE U.S. DEFENDERS EXPERIENCED MORTARS AND SHELLS BURSTING AROUND THEM ALL DAY ON DECEMBER 22, ONE OF THEM SERIOUSLY WOUNDING MAJOR PARKER. AS A RESULT, MAJ. ELLIOTT C. GOLDSTEIN TOOK OVER COMMAND.

BUT IN THE PREDAWN OF DECEMBER 23, A REGIMENT FROM THE 2ND SS HIT THEM HARD. THEY FOUGHT OFF THE GERMAN ASSAULT, BUT THEY KNEW MORE WOULD COME.

THAT EVENING, JUST AS IT WAS GETTING DARK, THE GERMANS BOMBARDED WHAT WAS NOW BEING CALLED "PARKER'S CROSSROADS" FOR 20 LONG MINUTES.

THEN THE FULL WEIGHT OF THE 2ND SS FELL ON BARAQUE DE FRAITURE.

THOSE WHO MANAGED TO ESCAPE FELL BACK TO BELLE HAIE AND MANHAY TO THE NORTHWEST.

THE ENEMY BROKE THROUGH. THE ROADBLOCK'S BEEN WIPED OUT!

MEANWHILE, A FEW MILES TO THE EAST, DESPERATE TROOPS WERE TRYING TO PULL OUT OF THE FORTIFIED GOOSE EGG.

AS USUAL, THE 112TH IS UNREPORTED, UNSUNG, AND UNRELIEVED.

AMONG THOSE TRYING TO ESCAPE THE POCKET WERE THE 7TH ARMORED DIVISION, THE 106TH DIVISION, THE 12TH CAVALRY GROUP, AND MEN FROM THE 112TH REGIMENT OF THE 28TH DIVISION TRYING TO HOLD A LINE TO THE SOUTH.

A HANDFUL OF LIGHT TANKS AND TANK DESTROYERS PROVIDED COVERING FIRE FOR THE 112TH AS THEY RETREATED ACROSS A BRIDGE ON THE SALM RIVER.

CLIMB ON, BOYS, THIS ONE'S GOING OUT.

ABOUT AN HOUR LATER, THE TANK DESTROYER PASSED A GROUP OF MEN DIGGING FOXHOLES.

ARE YOU LOOKING FOR SOMEPLACE SAFE?

YEAH, IF THAT'S POSSIBLE.

WELL, BUDDY, JUST PARK YOUR VEHICLE BEHIND US.

WE'RE THE 82ND AIRBORNE, AND THIS IS AS FAR AS THE BASTARDS ARE GOING.

EVERYONE HAD BEEN PULLED OUT OF THE GOOSE EGG.

ON THE MORNING OF DECEMBER 24, A HEAVY FOG BLANKETED MME. MARTHE MONRIQUE'S PLEASANT CAF , THE PAVILLON ARDENNAIS. AT ABOUT 0600, SHE HEARD AN EXPLOSION AND NOTICED THAT A GERMAN TANK HAD HIT AN AMERICAN PLANTED MINE.

HOW MANY KILOMETERS TO DINANT?

PAVILLON ARDENNAIS

ABOUT 10 KILOMETERS.

GOOD, WHAT ABOUT THE ROAD?

THE AMERICANS MINED THE WHOLE ROAD. THEY'VE BEEN WORKING ON IT DAY AND NIGHT . . .

. . . AND THERE ARE ABOUT 1,000 AMERICAN SOLDIERS HIDING JUST OVER THAT HILL.

THE GERMANS BELIEVED HER STORY, SO THEY PULLED THEIR TANKS OVER INTO A NEARBY WOODS AND CUT OFF THEIR ENGINES. MARTHE THEN SNUCK OUT HER BACK DOOR TO HIDE IN A NEIGHBOR'S CELLAR.

AT 1330, MATTHEW RIDGWAY'S MEN PULLED OUT OF THE GOOSE EGG. FOLLOWING MONTGOMERY'S DIRECTIVES, HE WAS PULLING THEM BACK FROM THE LINE, BUT MAJ. GEN. JIM GAVIN, COMMANDER OF THE 82ND AIRBORNE, PROTESTED STRONGLY.

THE 82ND HAS NEVER RETREATED, AND I DON'T LIKE THE IDEA OF STARTING NOW!

RIDGWAY WAS IN AGREEMENT. DESPITE MONTGOMERY'S ORDERS, HE SAT DOWN AND WROTE A PROCLAMATION TO HIS SUBORDINATES.

TO MY SUBORDINATES

IN MY OPINION THIS IS THE DYING GASP OF THE GERMAN ARMY. HE IS PUTTING EVERYTHING HE HAS INTO THIS FIGHT. WE ARE GOING TO SMASH THAT FINAL DRIVE HERE TODAY IN THIS CORPS ZONE. THIS COMMAND IS THE COMMAND THAT WILL SMASH THE GERMAN OFFENSIVE SPIRIT FOR THIS WAR. IMPRESS ON EVERY MAN IN YOUR DIVISIONS WITH THAT SPIRIT. WE ARE GOING TO LICK THE GERMANS HERE TODAY.

MAJ. GEN. MATTHEW RIDGWAY, COMMANDER, XVII AIRBORNE CORPS

AT ALMOST THE SAME TIME, MONTGOMERY WAS LECTURING U.S. FIRST ARMY CMDR. COURTNEY HODGES ON THE NECESSITY TO PULL BACK. THE BRITISH FIELD MARSHAL PROMISED BRITISH DIVISIONS WERE COMING DOWN FROM THE NORTH TO "SAVE" THE SITUATION. AFTER MONTGOMERY LEFT, HODGES TALKED WITH HIS STAFF.

HODGES HAD BEEN IN THE ARMY SINCE 1906 AND HAD SERVED WITH GEORGE MARSHALL IN THE PHILIPPINES AND GEORGE PATTON IN MEXICO. HIS FIRST ARMY WAS THE FIRST TROOPS TO REACH PARIS.

I DON'T LIKE THE IDEA OF FIGHTING A BATTLE BY BACKING OFF. COLLINS AND HARMON WON'T, EITHER.

MEANWHILE, A PATROL OF THE 2ND ARMORED DIVISION WAS NEAR CELLES, NOT FAR FROM MARTHE MONRIQUE'S CAFÉ.

THERE'S A BUNCH OF KRAUT TANKS, WE THINK FROM THE 2ND PANZER DIVISION . . .

. . . SOME BELGIAN CIVILIANS SAY THEY THINK THEY'RE ALMOST OUT OF GAS.

71

DURING THE NIGHT OF DECEMBER 23, A CAPTURED AMERICAN JEEP DRIVEN BY THREE GERMAN SCOUTS NEARED THE MEUSE RIVER BRIDGE AT DINANT . . .

. . . IT HIT A MINE, AND THE THREE OCCUPANTS WERE KILLED.

NOT LONG AFTER, A SINGLE PANZER IV TANK NEARED THE BRIDGE BUT WAS KNOCKED OUT BY AN UNKNOWN ASSAILANT. TWO PANTHERS WERE SOON ANNIHILATED.

THE KILLERS WERE A GROUP OF BRITISH SHERMAN FIREFLIES, WAITING SILENTLY FOR TARGETS AND MAKING SURE THAT THE 2ND PANZER DIVISION WOULD ADVANCE NO FARTHER.

HIGH WATER MARK

ON THE MORNING OF CHRISTMAS EVE, GERMAN UNITS WERE POUNDING AMERICAN UNITS ALL ALONG THE ROAD JUNCTIONS OF THE TAILLES PLATEAU:

VERDENNE,

HOTTON,

SOY,

AND MANHAY.

THE BATTLE FOR THE GRANDMÉNIL AREA IN MANHAY WAS ESPECIALLY VIOLENT. THE 2ND SS PANZER DIVISION WANTED TO CAPTURE THE TOWN BECAUSE BEYOND IT WAS ON THE ROAD LEADING DIRECTLY TO LIEGE. THE FIRST TANK IN THE ATTACKING COLUMN WAS A CAPTURED SHERMAN, SO THE AMERICANS DEFENDING THE TOWN, MADE UP OF ELEMENTS OF THE 3RD AND 7TH ARMORED DIVISION, THOUGHT THAT IT WAS ONE OF THEIR OWN U.S. UNITS WITHDRAWING.

THEN THE GERMANS BEGAN FIRING FLARES, AND THE AMERICAN DEFENDERS WERE SURPRISED TO FIND THE PANZERS RIGHT ON TOP OF THEM.

AS THE GERMANS PUSHED THROUGH GRANDM NIL, A LONE BAZOOKAMAN KNOCKED OUT THEIR LEAD TANK ON A ROAD BORDERED BY STEEP SLOPES, STOPPING THEIR ADVANCE OF THE 2ND SS FOR THE MOMENT.

ELEMENTS OF THE 75TH INFANTRY DIVISION THREW UP A LINE IN FRONT OF THE 2ND SS, RESTRICTING THE MOVEMENT OF THE GERMAN FORCES. THE BATTLE WOULD GO ON INTO CHRISTMAS DAY, WITH NEITHER SIDE GAINING THE ADVANTAGE.

AT 1430 ON CHRISTMAS EVE, GENERAL HARMON, COMMANDER OF THE 2ND ARMORED, CALLED J. LAWTON COLLINS'S HEADQUARTERS.

FOR THE NEXT FEW HOURS, THE MESSAGES SHOT BACK IN FORTH. WHO HAD THE AUTHORITY TO ALLOW HARMON TO MAKE HIS ATTACK? WHAT DID THE ORDERS MEAN? THE LOCATIONS AND DIRECTIVES WERE GARBLED AND MISUNDERSTOOD.

MY PATROLS HAVE SPOTTED LARGE CONCENTRATIONS OF GERMAN TANKS NEAR CELLES . . .

. . . YOU'VE GOT TO GIVE ME PERMISSION TO ATTACK THEM!

VII CO HEADQU

BUT HE'S NOT HERE, GENERAL HARMON.

FINALLY, COLLINS PUT OUT A CLEAR ORDER: HARMON'S 2ND ARMORED DIVISION WAS TO ATTACK THE GERMAN TANKS OF THE 2ND PANZER DIVISION ON THE MORNING OF CHRISTMAS DAY.

THE BASTARDS ARE IN THE BAG . . . THE KRAUTS ARE IN THE BAG!

8 MILES TO THE EAST, IN A CHÂTEAU NEAR LA ROCHE, BARON VON MANTEUFFEL, COMMANDER OF THE 5TH PANZER ARMY, WAS ON THE PHONE WITH COL. GEN. ALFRED JODL AT HITLER'S HEADQUARTERS.

. . . BY NOT TAKING BASTOGNE, OUR ADVANCE HAS BEEN TOO SLOW ON SECONDARY ROADS. THE AMERICANS HAVE HAD TIME TO BRING UP MORE AND FRESHER UNITS.

THE TIME HAS COME FOR A NEW PLAN. WE CAN REACH THE MEUSE, BUT THAT IS ALL WE CAN DO . . .

TWO FORMER SOLDIERS OF THE BELGIAN ARMY AND NEARBY BRITISH TROOPS PINPOINTED THE GERMANS AROUND THE VILLAGE OF FOY NOTRE DAME.

BRITISH FIREFLIES OF THE 29TH ARMORED BRIGADE CLOSED IN FROM THE WEST.

GENERAL HARMON WAS GETTING READY FOR THEIR ATTACK WHEN HE SPOTTED A SWAN, SERENELY GLIDING ACROSS THE SURFACE OF A NEARBY POND.

HEY, LOOK AT THAT!

HE TURNED TO HIS JEEP DRIVER.

TAKE YOUR CARBINE AND SHOOT THAT THING, AND GIVE IT TO THE MESS SERGEANT . . . THAT'S DINNER FOR TONIGHT.

THE 2ND PANZER HAD BY FAR OUTDISTANCED THE OTHER UNITS IN THE GERMAN OFFENSIVE. THEY HAD BEEN LUCKY IN CAPTURING BRIDGES INTACT, UNLIKE THEIR NEXT NEAREST PANZER UNITS, THE 116TH PANZER TO THE NORTHEAST AND THE PANZER LEHR TO THEIR SOUTH. BUT THEY WERE VERY STRUNG OUT, THE MEN WERE EXHAUSTED, AND THEY WERE VERY SHORT OF GAS.

AS THE TANKS OF THE 2ND ARMORED ADVANCED TOWARD THE 2ND PANZER, THEY NOTICED LITTLE OBSERVATION PLANES, PIPER CUBS, FLYING AHEAD OF THEM.

THESE WERE ARTILLERY OBSERVERS OF THE DIVISION ARTILLERY, WHO WERE DIRECTING BRITISH TYPHOON FIGHTER-BOMBERS TO THEIR TARGETS.

THE ADVANCING TANKERS WERE TREATED TO A GRATIFYING FIREWORKS SHOW.

THE BATTLE BETWEEN THE 2ND ARMORED AND THE 2ND PANZER WAS A MOSAIC OF HUNDREDS OF VIOLENT LITTLE FIGHTS BETWEEN GROUPS OF TANKS WITH VERY FEW FIGHTS BETWEEN SINGLE TANKS.

JUST AS THE GERMANS HAD LEARNED ON THE EASTERN FRONT IN RUSSIA, TANK FIGHTS IN CLOSE QUARTERS PUT LESS POWERFUL TANKS ON EQUAL FOOTING WITH THEIR LARGER, MORE POWERFUL OPPONENTS.

THE PANZER LEHR DIVISION MADE AN ATTEMPT TO AID THE 2ND PANZER FROM THE SOUTH, BUT THEY WERE STOPPED BY P-38 FIGHTER-BOMBERS.

THE 116TH PANZER TRIED TO RESCUE THEM FROM THE EAST, BUT THEY WERE BLOCKED BY THE 84TH INFANTRY DIVISION AT VERDENNE AND HOTTON.

IT WAS A BLOODY, CONFUSING FIGHT BETWEEN INFANTRY AND TANKS THAT CONVINCED BOTH SIDES THAT THEY HAD LOST.

THAT EVENING, HARMON AND HIS STAFF GOT A CHANCE TO EAT THE SWAN. THEY FOUND IT "DELICIOUSLY DUCKLIKE" AND STRIPPED IT CLEAN.

SOUTH OF BASTOGNE, THE 4TH ARMORED DIVISION WAS PUSHING NORTH WITH THE 37TH TANK BATTALION IN THE LEAD. ITS COMMANDER, COL. CREIGHTON ABRAMS, ROLLED AHEAD IN HIS SHERMAN "THUNDERBOLT IV."

AHEAD WERE THE VILLAGE OF ASSENOIS AND TWO 88MM GUNS. PVT. JAMES HENDRIX, A RED-HEADED KID FROM ARKANSAS, JUMPED OUT OF HIS HALF-TRACK AND CHARGED AHEAD, HIS M1 BLAZING, SCREAMING AT THE TOP OF HIS LUNGS.

AS HE RAN AND YELLED, HE FIRED ON THE CREWS OF THE 88S, UNNERVING THEM.

HE SHOT ONE GERMAN, BUTT-STROKED ANOTHER WITH THE STOCK OF HIS RIFLE, AND CHARGED ON.

THE CREWS OF THE 88S CAME OUT OF THEIR POSITION WITH THEIR HANDS HELD HIGH, THEIR EYES WIDE WITH FEAR. FOR THIS ACTION ABOVE AND BEYOND THE CALL OF DUTY, HENDRIX WAS AWARDED THE MEDAL OF HONOR.

LIEUTENANT CHARLES BOGGESS LED HIS NINE TANKS THROUGH THE VILLAGE. HIS OWN TANK FIRED 21 ROUNDS ON THE WAY THROUGH, NOT TAKING ANY CHANCES WHEN SOMETHING LOOKED SUSPICIOUS.

AT 16, JUST AS IT WAS GETTING DARK, HE SAW SOME FOXHOLES AHEAD. NOT KNOWING IF THEY BELONGED TO FRIEND OR FOE, HE STOOD UP IN HIS TURRET AND YELLED.

HEY, COME HERE! THIS IS THE 4TH ARMORED.

A DIRTY BUT GRINNING PARATROOPER WALKED OVER TO HIM.

I'M LIEUTENANT WEBSTER OF THE 326TH ENGINEERS, OF THE 101ST AIRBORNE . . . GLAD TO SEE YOU.

PATTON PACKED HIS FORCES IN THE NARROW CORRIDOR, AND MEN OF THE 101ST AND THE OTHER UNITS TRAPPED IN THE POCKET ATTACKED TO BROADEN THEIR PERIMETER. GENERAL MAXWELL TAYLOR, THE COMMANDER OF THE 101ST WHO HAD BEEN IN WASHINGTON, D.C., WHEN THE GERMAN OFFENSIVE BEGAN, ARRIVED IN BASTOGNE ON DECEMBER 27. WHEN HE MET GENERAL McAULIFFE HE SHOOK HIS HAND AND SAID . . .

EVERYBODY'S BEEN WORRIED ABOUT YOU. JUST WHAT IS THE CONDITION OF THE DIVISION?

NO REASON TO WORRY ABOUT US. WE'RE READY TO ATTACK.

HITLER WAS INFORMED OF THESE EVENTS, BUT HE STILL REFUSED TO GIVE UP THE OBJECTIVE OF ANTWERP.

WE MUST CAPTURE BASTOGNE.

SUCCESS OR FAILURE EAST OR WEST OF THE MEUSE HINGES ON THE CAPTURE OF CRUCIAL CROSSROADS . . .

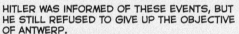

AROUND MIDNIGHT ON DECEMBER 27, GEN. ERNEST HARMON SAT IN A HALF-DESTROYED FARMHOUSE NEAR CELLES AND WROTE A REPORT TO GENERALS HODGES AND COLLINS. HE STATED THAT THE 2ND ARMORED HAD KILLED OR WOUNDED SOME 2,500 GERMANS AND CAPTURED 1,200. THEY HAD DESTROYED 405 VEHICLES, TANKS, AND ASSAULT GUNS AND DESTROYED 75 HEAVY GUNS.

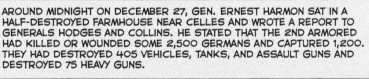

HARMON FELT LITTLE JOY. IT HAD BEEN A GREAT SLAUGHTER OF THE ENEMY, BUT THE AMERICANS HAD LOST A LOT OF MEN, TOO.

DEATH RATTLE

IT WILL PROBABLY NEVER BE KNOWN HOW MANY OF SKORZENY'S COMMANDOS MANAGED TO COMPLETE THEIR MISSIONS. ONLY 18 WERE CAPTURED AND SHOT, AND 3 MADE IT BACK TO GERMAN LINES. COUNTLESS OTHERS WERE DOUBTLESS KILLED IN BATTLE.

BUT ONE THING IS FOR SURE: THE CONFUSION THEY CAUSED MORE THAN MADE UP FOR ANY LACK OF CONTRIBUTIONS IN BATTLE. THEY HAD EVERY G.I. WONDERING WHO WAS A FRIEND OR FOE.

WHAT'S THE CAPITAL OF DELAWARE?

WHO CARES?

HITLER SENT THE 1ST SS PANZER DIVISION SOUTH, FIRST FOR A SHORT REST AND REFITTING IN THE ST. VITH AREA AND THEN ON DOWN TO BASTOGNE TO TRY TO CRACK THE ROADBLOCK.

TO COUNTER THIS, PATTON THREW IN THE VETERAN 35TH INFANTRY DIVISION BETWEEN THE 4TH ARMORED AND 26TH INFANTRY. ON THE NORTHERN SHOULDER, THE POWERFUL 6TH ARMORED DIVISION WAS PUT INTO THE LINE WITH ITS 185 TANKS.

THE BASTOGNE CORRIDOR WAS NOW WIDE AND STRONG ENOUGH TO WITHDRAW ALL THE WOUNDED TO HOSPITALS IN THE REAR LINES. AMMUNITION, FOOD, AND WINTER CLOTHING WERE PROVIDED.

J. LAWTON COLLINS WANTED TO MOUNT AN OFFENSIVE BY DECEMBER 31, BUT MONTGOMERY AGAIN WARNED AGAINST IT. COURTNEY HODGES FINALLY MADE THE POINT FOR THE VII CORPS COMMANDER.

MARSHAL, WE DON'T DO THINGS LIKE YOU BRITISH. IN AN OPERATION LIKE THIS, WE REGROUP ON THE LINE OF ATTACK.

ALL ALONG THE LINE, BOTH NORTH AND SHOUTH, OFFENSIVES BEGAN, BOTH GERMAN AND AMERICAN, AND COLLIDED INTO EACH OTHER.

TO VON RUNDSTEDT AND MODEL, IT WAS NO LONGER A FIGHT TO REACH ANTWERP. THEY WERE NOW FACING 38 ALLIED DIVISIONS IN THE ARDENNES. IT WAS NOW A SIMPLE CASE OF "GOING OVER TO THE DEFENSE EVERYWHERE."

HITLER HIMSELF FIXATED ON ANOTHER IMPOSSIBLE OBSESSION: TO DESTROY THE SMALL MARKET TOWN OF BASTOGNE.

BUT HITLER DID HAVE ONE SURPRISE UP HIS SLEEVE: OPERATION BASEPLATE. ON NEW YEAR'S DAY, 1945, 875 GERMAN SINGLE-ENGINE PLANES TOOK OFF FROM AIRFIELDS ALL OVER WESTERN GERMANY. THEIR MISSION WAS TO ATTACK BRITISH AND AMERICAN AIRFIELDS ALL OVER BELGIUM AND HOLLAND AND TO INFLICT DAMAGE ON SCORES OF ALLIED FIGHTERS. THIS GERMAN ATTACK INCLUDED 21 NEW ME 262 JET FIGHTERS, THE WORLD'S FIRST OPERATIONAL COMBAT JETS.

MORE THAN 200 ALLIED AIRCRAFT WERE DESTROYED IN BASEPLATE, BUT THE LUFTWAFFE LOST A STAGGERING 300 AIRCRAFT.

BY THIS POINT IN THE WAR, THE BRITISH AND AMERICANS COULD SUSTAIN THESE KINDS OF LOSSES, BUT THE GERMANS COULD NOT.

THE FIGHTING DIDN'T GET ANY EASIER FOR EITHER SIDE, ESPECIALLY FOR MAJ. GEN. CHARLES KILBURN'S 11TH ARMORED DIVISION.

ATTACKING FROM A POSITION WEST OF BASTOGNE, FROM DECEMBER 31 THROUGH JANUARY 3 THE DIVISION LOST 661 MEN KILLED, WOUNDED, AND MISSING.

IN THAT SAME PERIOD OF TIME, THEY LOST 53 TANKS.

MAYBE IT WAS BECAUSE OF THEIR EXPERIENCES THAT MEN OF THE 11TH ARMORED MURDERED 60 UNARMED GERMAN PRISONERS OF WAR AT THE VILLAGE CHENOGNE ON NEW YEAR'S DAY. MAYBE IT WAS RETALIATION FOR MALMEDY.

MORE AND MORE ALLIED DIVISIONS WERE BROUGHT IN TO BEAT THE BULGE BACK TO WHERE IT HAD STARTED. THIS PERIOD OF THE BATTLE WAS, IN MANY WAYS, THE MOST DIFFICULT. ONE REASON WAS THAT THE WEATHER GOT MUCH COLDER, AND IN MANY PLACES, THE SNOW WAS TWO TO THREE FEET DEEP.

ANOTHER REASON WAS THAT THE GERMANS, WHO WERE NOW FALLING BACK, WOULD OCCUPY TOWNS AND VILLAGES IN BELGIUM AND LUXEMBOURG.

THE GERMANS, NOW NESTLED INSIDE WARM VILLAGES, COULD DEFEND HANDILY AGAINST THE COLD AMERICANS, WHO HAD TO DIG THEM OUT.

TO ACCOMPLISH THIS, U.S. UNITS FREQUENTLY HAD TO BOMB AND SHELL THE TOWNS UNTIL THEY WERE SHATTERED RUINS.

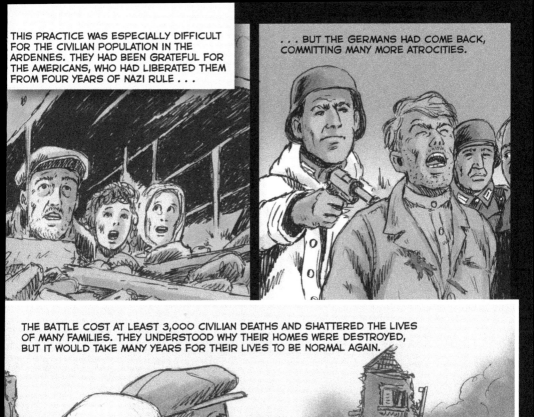

THIS PRACTICE WAS ESPECIALLY DIFFICULT FOR THE CIVILIAN POPULATION IN THE ARDENNES. THEY HAD BEEN GRATEFUL FOR THE AMERICANS, WHO HAD LIBERATED THEM FROM FOUR YEARS OF NAZI RULE . . .

. . . BUT THE GERMANS HAD COME BACK, COMMITTING MANY MORE ATROCITIES.

THE BATTLE COST AT LEAST 3,000 CIVILIAN DEATHS AND SHATTERED THE LIVES OF MANY FAMILIES. THEY UNDERSTOOD WHY THEIR HOMES WERE DESTROYED, BUT IT WOULD TAKE MANY YEARS FOR THEIR LIVES TO BE NORMAL AGAIN.

ON JANUARY 3, ALL AMERICAN FORCES WITH THE BRITISH XXX CORPS ATTACKED AGAINST THE WESTERN TIP.

THE FIGHTING ON THE NORTHERN SIDE OF THE BASTOGNE CORRIDOR WAS PARTICULARLY VIOLENT. ELEMENTS OF THE 101ST AIRBORNE AND THE 10TH ARMORED SMASHED AGAINST THE 9TH AND 12TH SS DIVISIONS THAT WERE THEMSELVES IN THE PROCESS OF ATTACKING.

TERRIBLE LOSSES ACCUMULATED ON BOTH SIDES.

THE AMERICAN SOLDIERS WHO FOUGHT IN THE BULGE WERE, IN MANY WAYS, A LOT DIFFERENT FROM THOSE WHO HAD LANDED IN NORMANDY AROUND D-DAY. IN THIS BATTLE, THEY HAD LEARNED TO GO WITHOUT THE AIR SUPPORT THAT THEY HAD TAKEN FOR GRANTED IN THE SUMMER AND FALL OF 1944. THEIR ENDLESS SUPPLY OF FOOD, AMMO, AND WARM CLOTHING WAS GONE.

THEY HAD LEARNED THE HUMILIATION OF DEFEAT . . . AND RETREAT. THEY SAW FEAR AND DEATH ALL AROUND THEM, AND THEY KNEW THAT IT COULD COME EASILY AND QUICKLY. THEY KNEW HOW IMPORTANT IT WAS TO KEEP THEIR FEET DRY AND THEIR RIFLES FROM FREEZING. BUT THE MOST IMPORTANT LESSON, THE LESSON THAT WOULD HAUNT THE SOLDIERS FOR THE REST OF THEIR LIVES, WAS THAT THEY HAD TO KILL WITHOUT REMORSE OR PITY.

ONE OF THE PRIMARY REASONS HITLER HAD LAUNCHED THE ARDENNES OFFENSIVE WAS TO DRIVE A WEDGE BETWEEN THE BRITISH AND AMERICAN ALLIES. IN ONE WAY, HE ALMOST DID. FIELD MARSHAL MONTGOMERY SENT A LETTER TO GENERAL EISENHOWER SUGGESTING THAT HE BE PUT IN CHARGE OF ALL THE WESTERN ALLIES; TO MANY, THIS IMPLIED THAT MONTGOMERY BELIEVED GENERAL BRADLEY WAS NOT UP TO THE ASSIGNMENT AND THAT EISENHOWER HAD USED BAD JUDGMENT IN ASSIGNING HIM TO THAT POSITION. THE LETTER MADE EISENHOWER SO FURIOUS THAT HE THREATENED TO RESIGN.

MONTGOMERY ALSO HELD A PRESS CONFERENCE FOR BRITISH NEWSPAPERS. COMING OUT OF THE PRESS CONFERENCE, A BRITISH JOURNALIST WROTE THAT MONTGOMERY HAD "FORESEEN THE OFFENSIVE, AND HAD SAVED THE AMERICANS."

IN BOTH CASES, MONTGOMERY HAD TO WRITE A LETTER OF APOLOGY, BUT STILL, THE COMMENTS AND ACCUSATIONS WERE OUT IN THE COURT OF PUBLIC OPINION. WHAT COULD BE DONE TO SMOOTH RUFFLED FEATHERS?

IT WOULD TAKE NONE OTHER THAN SIR WINSTON CHURCHILL TO SMOOTH THINGS OVER IN A SPEECH IN THE HOUSE OF COMMONS: "THE AMERICANS HAVE ENGAGED 30 TO 40 MEN FOR EVERY ONE WE HAVE ENGAGED AND THEY HAVE LOST 60 TO 80 MEN FOR EVERY ONE OF US. IT WAS THE GREATEST AMERICAN BATTLE OF THE WAR AND WILL, I BELIEVE, BE REGARDED AS AN EVER-FAMOUS AMERICAN VICTORY."

FROM NORTH TO SOUTH, THE AMERICANS CONTINUED TO POUND THE GERMAN FORCES IN EARLY JANUARY 1945. HAVING LOST MOST OF THEIR TANKS, THE WEHRMACHT WAS FORCED TO DEFEND LITTLE POCKETS OR VILLAGES. HITLER FINALLY, AND GRUDGINGLY, GAVE HIS PERMISSION TO WITHDRAW FROM THE BULGE. MANY OF THESE FORCES WOULD ESCAPE FUTURE ENCIRCLEMENT FROM ALLIED FORCES, RETREATING BEHIND THE SIEGFRIED LINE.

AT 0905 ON THE MORNING OF JANUARY 16, 1945, ELEMENTS OF THE 11TH ARMORED DIVISION, PART OF PATTON'S THIRD ARMY, INFANTRYMEN OF THE 2ND ARMORED DIVISION, AND PART OF HODGE'S FIRST ARMY MET NEAR THE TOWN OF HOUFFALIZE. IT HAD TAKEN THESE MEN TWO WEEKS TO CLOSE A 22-MILE GAP. THEY HAD FOUGHT THE GERMANS EVERY INCH OF THE WAY.

ON THAT DAY, IT WAS ANNOUNCED THAT THE BATTLE OF THE BULGE WAS OFFICIALLY OVER.

THIS SEEMS RATHER ODD, FOR THE AMERICANS HAD NOT YET REACHED THE LINE FROM WHERE THE GERMANS HAD BEGUN THEIR GREAT OFFENSIVE. BUT HISTORIANS WOULD ALWAYS TELL THAT STORY AS PART OF THE GENERAL OFFENSIVE THAT WOULD TAKE AMERICAN FORCES INTO GERMANY AND ON TO BERLIN LATER THAT SPRING.

ON THE AFTERNOON OF JANUARY 23, BRIG. GEN. BRUCE CLARKE LED HIS COMBAT COMMAND B AND THE 7TH ARMORED DIVISION, BACK INTO THE RUINS OF ST. VITH.

ON THE OTHER SIDE OF EUROPE IN POLAND, COL. HURLEY FULLER, WHO HAD COMMANDED THE 110TH REGIMENT OF THE 28TH DIVISION AT CLERVAUX, WAS IN A GERMAN PRISONER-OF-WAR CAMP.

HE AND HIS MEN COULD HEAR THE CANNON FIRE FROM THE ADVANCING RUSSIAN RED ARMY.

"WATCH ON THE RHINE" WAS CRAWLING BACK TO THE FATHERLAND LIKE A GREAT, WOUNDED, BLEEDING BEAST. FEW OF THOSE WHO SURVIVED THAT RETREAT BELIEVED THERE WAS THE SLIGHTEST CHANCE OF GERMAN VICTORY.

ON MAY 7, 1945, GERMANY SURRENDERED.

DURING THE BATTLE OF THE BULGE, THE U.S. ARMY REPORTED 89,98_
CASUALTIES: 10,276 KILLED; 47,493 WOUNDED; AND 23,218 MISSING. TH_
BRITISH SUFFERED 1,408 BATTLE CASUALTIES, WHICH INCLUDED 200 DEAD_

THE ACCEPTED GERMAN FIGURE IS 81,834, WHICH INCLUDED 12,652 DEAD, 38,600 WOUNDED, AND 30,582 MISSING. IN RETROSPECT, THE GERMANS WOULD HAVE DONE BETTER IF THEY HAD STAYED BEHIND THEIR GUNS AND PILLBOXES IN THE SIEGFRIED LINE— BY DOING THAT, THEY WOULD HAVE INFLICTED MORE CASUALTIES ON THE AMERICANS. BUT THE MARCH TO BERLIN, AND THE END OF WORLD WAR II, WAS INEVITABLE.

AFTER THE WAR, THE PEOPLE OF BELGIUM AND LUXEMBOURG BEGAN THE PROCESS OF REBUILDING THEIR HOMES AND VILLAGES. THE MARSHALL PLAN, WHICH BEGAN IN 1948, WAS AN AMERICAN INITIATIVE TO AID AND REBUILD WAR-DEVASTATED EUROPE, MODERNIZE AND BUILD EUROPEAN INDUSTRY AND TRADE, AND PREVENT THE SPREAD OF SOVIET COMMUNISM.

BUT THE ACTUAL BUILDING PART WAS STILL THE RESPONSIBILITY OF LOCAL CITIZENS. THE LITTLE TOWN OF HOUFFALIZE WAS DESTROYED SO THOROUGHLY THAT THEY CRUSHED DOWN THE RUBBLE FROM THE BATTLE AND REBUILT THE TOWN 3 METERS HIGHER THAN IT WAS ORIGINALLY.

TODAY, THE ARDENNES IS A BEAUTIFUL AND PROSPEROUS REGION WITH BOOMING TIMBER AND TOURISM INDUSTRIES. VISITORS FROM ALL OVER EUROPE COME TO HUNT, FISH, CAMP, AND CANOE THE SWIFT AND BEAUTIFUL RIVERS AND TO EAT GOOD FOOD IN THE MANY RESTAURANTS AND INNS.

THE LOCALS TRULY LOVE AMERICANS AND ARE DELIGHTED TO WELCOME BACK OLD, WHITE-HAIRED MEN WHO ONCE DID THE UNBELIEVABLE IN THE WINTER OF 1944 AND 1945.

THIS SPECIAL RELATIONSHIP BETWEEN THE PEOPLE OF THE ARDENNES AND THE UNITED STATES IS ILLUSTRATED IN THE STORY OF STAFF SGT. HASSELL C. WHITFIELD. DURING THE GERMAN BOMBARDMENT OF THE LUXEMBOURGIAN VILLAGE OF OBERWAMPACH, WHITFIELD SOUGHT SHELTER IN THE CELLAR OF THE SCHILLING FAMILY. WHEN THE HOUSE CAUGHT FIRE, FIVE-YEAR-OLD MARCEL SCHILLING PANICKED AND RAN INTO THE EXPLODING STREET. WITHOUT HESITATION, WHITFIELD RAN AFTER HIM, SCOOPED HIM UP IN HIS ARMS, AND ATTEMPTED TO CARRY HIM TO SAFETY IN A NEIGHBOR'S DOORWAY. BEFORE HE REACHED SHELTER A SHELL EXPLODED, KILLING BOTH SOLDIER AND CHILD.

AT THE CHURCH IN OBERWAMPACH, THERE IS A MEMORIAL TABLET HONORING THE SOLDIER WHO GAVE HIS LIFE TRYING TO SAVE A CHILD.

MAYBE THAT SAYS IT ALL.

ALLIED AND AXIS DIVISIONS

US DIVISIONS

2ND ARMORED "HELL ON WHEELS"
3RD ARMORED "SPEARHEAD"
4TH ARMORED "NAME ENOUGH"
6TH ARMORED "SUPER SIXTH"
7TH ARMORED "LUCKY SEVENTH"
8TH ARMORED "IRON SNAKE"
9TH ARMORED "PHANTOM"
10TH ARMORED "TIGER"
82ND AIRBORNE "ALL-AMERICAN"
101ST AIRBORNE "SCREAMING
   EAGLES"
1ST INFANTRY "BIG RED ONE"
4TH INFANTRY "IVY"
5TH INFANTRY "RED DIAMOND"
26TH INFANTRY "YANKEE"
28TH INFANTRY "KEYSTONE"
30TH INFANTRY "OLD HICKORY"
35TH INFANTRY "SANTA FE"
75TH INFANTRY
80TH INFANTRY "BLUE RIDGE"
84TH INFANTRY "RAILSPLITTERS"
106TH INFANTRY "GOLDEN LION"

BRITISH DIVISIONS

GUARDS ARMOURED
29TH ARMOURED
43RD INFANTRY
51ST INFANTRY
53RD INFANTRY

GERMAN DIVISIONS

1ST SS PANZER "LIEBSTANDARTE
   SS ADOLF HITLER"
2ND SS PANZER "DAS REICH"
9TH SS PANZER "HOHENSTAUFEN"
12TH SS PANZER "HITLERJUGEND"
FÜHRERBEGLEIT BRIGADE (+)
FÜHRER GRENADIER BRIGADE (+)
PANZER LEHR
2ND PANZER
9TH PANZER
116TH PANZER
3RD PANZERGRENADIER
15TH PANZERGRENADIER
3RD FALLSCHIRMJÄGER
5TH FALLSCHIRMJÄGER
9TH INFANTRY
12TH INFANTRY
18TH INFANTRY
26TH INFANTRY
89TH INFANTRY
62ND VOLKSGRENADIER
79TH VOLKSGRENADIER
167TH VOLKSGRENADIER
212TH VOLKSGRENADIER
246TH VOLKSGRENADIER
276TH VOLKSGRENADIER
277TH VOLKSGRENADIER
326TH VOLKSGRENADIER
340TH VOLKSGRENADIER
352ND VOLKSGRENADIER
560TH VOLKSGRENADIER

U.S. TANKS

M4A3 SHERMAN

CREW: 5
WEIGHT IN TONS: 30
MAIN GUN: 75MM

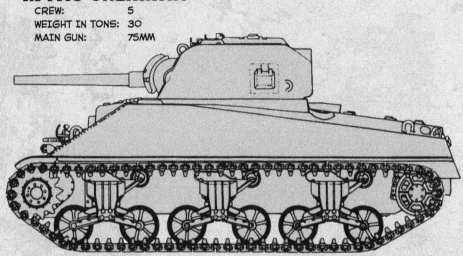

M4A1 SHERMAN

CREW: 5
WEIGHT IN TONS: 30
MAIN GUN: 76MM

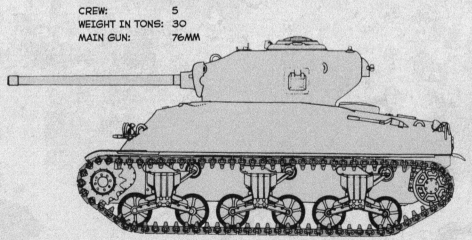

M5A1 STUART

CREW: 4
WEIGHT IN TONS: 15
MAIN GUN: 37MM

M18 HELLCAT TANK DESTROYER

CREW: 5
WEIGHT IN TONS: 17
MAIN GUN: 76MM

M3A1 HALF-TRACK

CREW: 13
WEIGHT IN TONS: 10
MAIN GUN: N/A

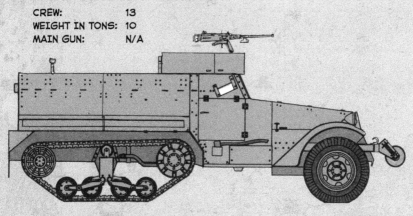

M10 TANK DESTROYER

CREW: 5
WEIGHT IN TONS: 30
MAIN GUN: 3 IN.

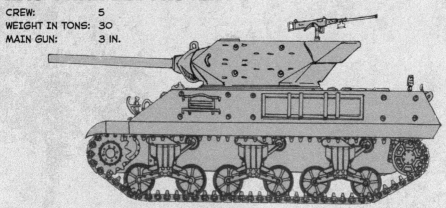

M36 TANK DESTROYER

CREW: 5
WEIGHT IN TONS: 28
MAIN GUN: 90MM

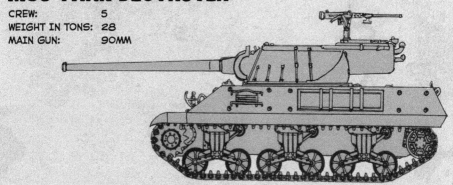

GERMAN TANKS

JAGDPANZER IV

CREW: 4
WEIGHT IN TONS: 24
MAIN GUN: 75MM

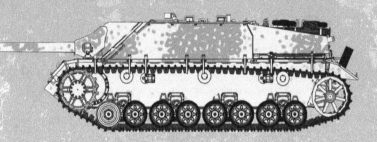

PANTHER

CREW: 5
WEIGHT IN TONS: 46
MAIN GUN: 75MM

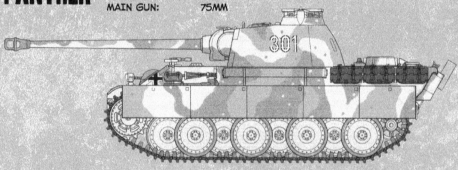

HETZER TANK DESTROYER

CREW: 4
WEIGHT IN TONS: 10
MAIN GUN: 75MM

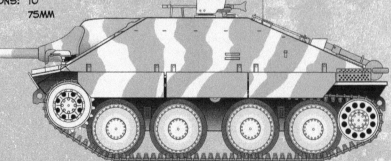

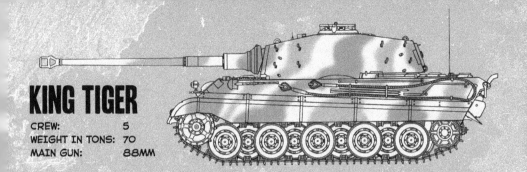

KING TIGER

CREW: 5
WEIGHT IN TONS: 70
MAIN GUN: 88MM

PANZER IV AUSF. J

CREW: 5
WEIGHT IN TONS: 25
MAIN GUN: 75MM

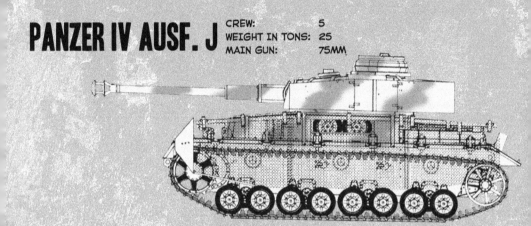

HANOMAG 251

CREW: 12
WEIGHT IN TONS: 9
MAIN GUN: N/A

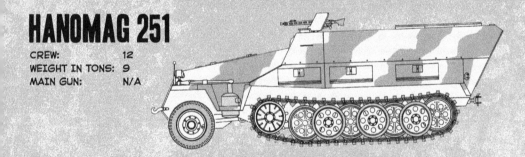

STUG III ASSAULT GUN

CREW: 4
WEIGHT IN TONS: 22
MAIN GUN: 75MM

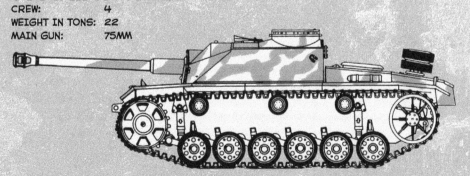

FURTHER READING

RICK ATKINSON, *THE GUNS AT LAST LIGHT: THE WAR IN WESTERN EUROPE, 1944–1945* (MACMILLAN)

JOHN BRUNING, *THE BATTLE OF THE BULGE: THE PHOTOGRAPHIC HISTORY OF AN AMERICAN TRIUMPH* (ZENITH PRESS)

MICHAEL COLLINS AND MARTIN KING, *VOICES OF THE BULGE: UNTOLD STORIES FROM VETERANS OF THE BATTLE OF THE BULGE* (ZENITH PRESS)

JOHN S. D. EISENHOWER, *THE BITTER WOODS: THE BATTLE OF THE BULGE* (DA CAPO PRESS)

MICHAEL GREEN AND JAMES D. BROWN, *WAR STORIES OF THE BATTLE OF THE BULGE* (ZENITH PRESS)

MAX HASTINGS, *ARMAGEDDON: THE BATTLE FOR GERMANY* (RANDOM HOUSE)

ALEX KERSHAW, *THE LONGEST WINTER: THE BATTLE OF THE BULGE AND THE EPIC STORY OF WWII'S MOST DECORATED PLATOON* (DA CAPO PRESS)

CHARLES B. MACDONALD, *A TIME FOR TRUMPETS: THE UNTOLD STORY OF THE BATTLE OF THE BULGE* (WILLIAM MORROW)

JOHN C. MCMANUS, *ALAMO IN THE ARDENNES: THE UNTOLD STORY OF THE AMERICAN SOLDIERS WHO MADE THE DEFENSE OF BASTOGNE POSSIBLE* (NAL TRADE)

DANNY PARKER, *BATTLE OF THE BULGE: HITLER'S ARDENNES OFFENSIVE, 1944–1945* (DA CAPO)

JOHN TOLAND, *BATTLE: THE STORY OF THE BULGE* (BISON BOOKS)

ABOUT THE AUTHOR

WRITER AND ARTIST WAYNE VANSANT WAS THE PRIMARY ARTIST
FOR MARVEL'S *THE 'NAM* FOR MORE THAN FIVE YEARS. SINCE
THEN, HE HAS WRITTEN AND ILLUSTRATED MANY HISTORICALLY
ACCURATE GRAPHIC HISTORIES SUCH AS *THE HAMMER AND THE
ANVIL*; *THE VIETNAM WAR: A GRAPHIC HISTORY*; *NORMANDY: A
GRAPHIC HISTORY OF D-DAY, THE ALLIED INVASION OF HITLER'S
FORTRESS EURPOPE*; AND *GETTYSBURG: THE GRAPHIC HISTORY
OF AMERICA'S MOST FAMOUS BATTLE AND THE TURNING POINT OF
THE CIVIL WAR*. HE RECENTLY PUBLISHED *GRANT VS. LEE*, *BOMBING
NAZI GERMANY*, AND *THE RED BARON* FOR ZENITH PRESS.

MORE GRAPHIC HISTORY BOOKS

FROM WAYNE VANSANT AND ZENITH PRESS

PRAISE FOR *NORMANDY*

"Highly recommended."
–*ArmchairGeneral.com*

"Vansant does an outstanding job of adding more details and making the events come alive."
–*Comic Buyers Guide*

"This book does a great job of bringing the events to life."
–*BookLegion*

PRAISE FOR *GETTYSBURG*

"This graphic account of the campaign and Battle of Gettysburg will appeal to experts and novices alike. It offers an accurate, fast-paced narrative with striking illustrations that dramatize the action and mark the course of the battle with vivid clarity."
–*James M. McPherson, Pulitzer Prize-winning historian of* Battle Cry of Freedom *and* Hallowed Ground: A Walk at Gettysburg

"*Gettysburg: The Graphic History* is a brilliant achievement. Writer/artist Wayne Vansant is at the top of his game with his graphic history of the battle known as "the high water mark of the Confederacy." It is an excellent, accessible visual account for a younger audience or those unfamiliar with the battle that inspired President Abraham Lincoln's greatest speech, the Gettysburg Address"
–*Dwight Jon Zimmerman, #1 New York Times best-selling co-author of* Lincoln's Last Days

Visit **zenithpress.com**